In this issue we consider three distinguished and very different careers.
Griffith Borgeson recounts the adventurous, heroic life of the late W.F. Bradley,
the most eminent automotive journalist in the English language.
There is an account of the wooden monocoque automobiles of Frank Costin,
that designer of flagrantly unconventional cars with superb aerodynamic properties.
Then, with the aid of a comprehensive selection of his drawings, Dan Burger evaluates
the legacy of designer Alan H. Leamy, whose most celebrated creation is the L-29 Cord.
We chronicle the development of two automotive tours de force, separated in time by more than fifty years.
First, there is a history of Knox, the first aircooled production car to be manufactured
in any significant quantity. Then Roy Query's photography highlights the Lotus 38
that Jimmy Clark drove to victory in the Indianapolis 500 of 1965.
For those who are fascinated by the aesthetic aspects of automotive history we explore
some trends in luxury coachbuilding during the years between 1909 and 1932,
and focus upon two exceptionally fine representatives of that period.
Rick Lenz's photographs capture the startling beauty of the 1930 Ruxton sedan,
whose lowness is dramatized by designer Josef Urban's bands of brilliant color.
Finally, we look briefly at the S.S.I Airline Saloon, one of Jaguar's precursors,
a car whose cautious concessions to streamlined design have drawn mixed reviews over the years.

# Automobile Quarterly

*The Connoisseur's Magazine of Motoring Today, Yesterday and Tomorrow*

Second Quarter 1982             Volume XX, Number 2

**PUBLISHER AND EDITOR IN CHIEF:**
L. SCOTT BAILEY

**EUROPEAN EDITOR:**
GRIFFITH BORGESON

**CONTRIBUTING EDITORS:**
ANGELO TITO ANSELMI, WILLIAM BODDY,
RUSS CATLIN, PAUL FRÈRE, ALLAN GIRDLER,
JEFFREY I. GODSHALL, KARL LUDVIGSEN,
JOHN B. MONTVILLE, GARY WITZENBURG

**ASSOCIATE EDITOR:**
MARGUERITE KELLY

**ASSISTANT EDITOR:**
WILLIAM ALAN COON

**STAFF ASSISTANT:**
MARGARET BUCHANAN BAILEY

**RESEARCH:**
HENRY AUSTIN CLARK, JR.

**RESEARCH ASSOCIATES:**
CHARLES L. BETTS, JR., U.S.A.,
NICHOLAS FRANCO, JR., SPAIN,
GIANNI ROGLIATTI, ITALY,
MICHAEL SEDGWICK, GREAT BRITAIN

**ART DIRECTORS:**
THOMAS C. HOUTZ, MICHAEL PARDO

**CHIEF PHOTOGRAPHER:**
ROY QUERY

**PHOTOGRAPHERS:**
DOUGLASS WHITFIELD BAILEY,
GIORGIO BELLIA, GIORGIO BOSCHETTI,
NEILL BRUCE, RICK LENZ,
CARL MALOTKA, STANLEY ROSENTHAL

**ARTISTS:**
JAMES ALLINGTON, WALTER GOTSCHKE,
PETER HELCK, YOSHIHIRO INOMOTO,
KEN RUSH

**PRODUCTION EDITOR:**
MARY B. WILLIAMS

**ADMINISTRATIVE ASSISTANT:**
HELEN M. FREER

**BUSINESS MANAGER:**
KEVIN G. BITZ

**VICE-PRESIDENT:**
MARGARET T. BAILEY

Automobile Quarterly is published quarterly by Automobile Quarterly, Inc., in association with the Princeton Institute for Historic Research. Editorial Offices: 221 Nassau Street, Princeton, New Jersey 08540. Office of Publication: 245 West Main Street, Kutztown, Pennsylvania 19530. Telephone: 215-683-8352. Automobile Quarterly is printed in the United States by the Kutztown Publishing Company on Mead Offset Enamel paper; color separations by Lincoln Graphics Incorporated, Cherry Hill, New Jersey; binding by National Publishing Company, Philadelphia, Pennsylvania. Single copies: $12.95. Annual subscriptions: $43.80, U.S.A.; $46.80, overseas. Four-Year Indexes (Volume I-IV, Volume V-VIII, Volume IX-XII and Volume XIII-XVI) are available at $12.95 each. All subscriptions, orders, changes of address and correspondence concerning subscriptions should be sent to 245 West Main Street, Kutztown, Pennsylvania 19530. Second class postage paid at Kutztown, Pennsylvania and at additional mailing offices.

© Automobile Quarterly, Inc., 1982. All rights reserved under Pan American and Universal Copyright Conventions by Automobile Quarterly, Inc. Reproduction without permission is prohibited. Library of Congress Catalog Card Number 62-4005. ISSN 0005-1438.

# CONTENTS

| | | | |
|---|---|---|---|
| 116 | KNOX: "THE PERFECT CAR"<br>BY JOHN J. KEEBLER III | 162 | W.F. BRADLEY: JOURNALIST, HISTORIAN, CATALYST<br>BY GRIFFITH BORGESON |
| 132 | THE CAREER AND THE CREATIONS OF ALAN H. LEAMY<br>BY DAN BURGER | 180 | THE WOODEN CHASSIS AUTOMOBILES OF FRANK COSTIN<br>BY DENNIS ORTENBURGER<br>PHOTOGRAPHY BY NEILL BRUCE |
| 144 | L-29 CORD CABRIOLET BY ALAN H. LEAMY: A COLOR PORTFOLIO<br>PHOTOGRAPHY BY ROY QUERY | 204 | THE GOLDEN AGE OF THE LUXURY CAR<br>BY PAUL BRENNAN<br>PHOTOGRAPHY BY ROY QUERY |
| 150 | "A GENUINE LOWNESS INGENIOUSLY ATTAINED": RUXTON<br>BY TOM MEREDITH<br>PHOTOGRAPHY BY RICK LENZ | 216 | STALKING A CHAMPION: JIM HAYNES AND HIS MYSTERY LOTUS<br>BY ED MORLEY<br>PHOTOGRAPHY BY ROY QUERY |
| 156 | PONTIAC'S INCREDIBLE GHOST CAR<br>BY KEN GROSS<br>PHOTOGRAPHY BY ROY QUERY | 222 | NOTES AND PHOTO CREDITS |
| | | 224 | COLOPHON |

Porsche, Krupp, DAF, Corvair and Volkswagen—make room for the pioneer aircooled automobiles: the Torbensen, Frayer-Miller, Eagle, Marmon, Franklin and Knox. Among all of these marques, it is Knox that holds the primacy as the first aircooled production car to be manufactured in significant quantities.

The florid literature produced by the Knox Automobile Company insisted that its product had other claims to preeminence. "Never before were motor cars placed on the market with such overwhelming assurance of the utmost reliability as the Knox," declared the company's 1904 catalog. "Certainly no other make has such a record of uninterrupted service." Indeed, the Knox was said by its producers to be the "perfect car." At the root of this perfection was the fact that it was "waterless"; there was nothing to freeze in bitterly cold weather, and the car's "automatic" air cooling prevented summer overheating.

Many people assume that watercooling, along with being more conventional, is also the older and more efficient means of maintaining thermal efficiency in an automobile engine. If we consider "normal" watercooled methods of heat dissipation as applied to automobiles, we realize that air is the greater medium into which the heat is finally absorbed. Water that circulates around the heat-producing sections of the engine is returned to the water-to-air heat exchanger, the common radiator. At the radiator the heat content of the cycled water comes into contact with healthy quantities of air, and is carried off. Air cooling eliminates the secondary medium of the water, its pumping apparatus and the radiator, with all of their complexity and weight.

The Volkswagen is to some people the first, and to others the only aircooled automobile. In reality it is neither. It is not even the first regular production automobile to be aircooled. One of the true pioneers in the field of aircooled cars was Henry A. Knox (1875-1957). Educated at the Springfield Technical Institute in Massachusetts before the turn of the century, Knox worked briefly with Duryea and served an apprenticeship with the Elektron Manufacturing Company, a producer of electrical equipment.

It was not an unusual beginning; many other early proponents of aircooling had backgrounds that included the development or construction of electrical equipment. Among them were Howard C. Marmon of the highly successful Marmon Automobile Company, Ferdinand Porsche, Josef Ganz, and John Wilkinson of the Franklin Automobile Company. Marmon's family owned a factory that manufactured heavy electrical equipment, and the young Marmon was given valuable factory floor space in the family concern for constructing one of his early prototype cars. Porsche was already working for an electrical firm in Vienna at fifteen, and was to remain there until he was twenty-three. One can only speculate about the relationship between these pioneers' early exposure to this form of technology and their later automotive designs.

While still a student at Springfield Technical Institute, Knox designed a four-cylinder aircooled gasoline engine and in 1897 undertook the building of experimental cars with the backing of A.H. Overman, a bicycle manufacturer of Chicopee Falls. Perhaps disappointed with the results or skeptical about the future of the automobile, Overman eventually withdrew his financial support, leaving Knox without a backer.

To the rescue came Elihu H. Cutler, Knox's former employer at Elektron Manufacturing. In 1900, while Knox was still in his mid-twenties, the Knox Automobile Company was launched, with a capitalization of $200,000. A few years later Cutler became the company's president after a disagreement with Knox, and the latter left the company. This type of falling out between early automobile designers and backers occurred frequently, and recalls the exit of Ransom Eli Olds from the Oldsmobile Company and the subsequent formation of his second auto company, REO. (See Automobile *Quarterly*, Volume XIV, Number 1). In similar fashion Knox quickly proceeded to form his own company, the

# KNOX:

# "THE PERFECT CAR"
## By John J. Keebler III

Knox Motor Truck Company. Later, due to legal pressure from the former Knox company, he changed its name to the Atlas Motor Truck Company. Then, between 1910 and 1945, Knox went on to design tanks and track-laying equipment for the U.S. government.

Knox's choice of aircooling, at such early points in the development of automotive technology and metallurgical engineering, seems both foolhardy and, in the face of results, ingenious. Knox was not alone in his experiments. Among his direct competitors was the Franklin Automobile Company, established in 1901. (See AUTOMOBILE *Quarterly*, Volume XVII, Number 3). Franklin would become one of the most successful producers of aircooled engines in America until Volkswagen came along in the early Fifties. In 1905 Franklin offered models with transversely mounted 1.7 liter engines with overhead valves, float-feed carburetors, two-speed planetary transmissions and wooden frames. Another aircooled competitor of Knox was Frayer-Miller, which resembled the watercooled automobiles of the time except for its use of a rotary fan to drive cooling air through an aluminum jacket around the cylinder. Another aircooled auto innovator, Marmon, joined many of the other early aircooled automobile builders, including Knox, in making extensive use of aluminum in the construction of their vehicles. So successful was the Marmon enterprise that the company was at one point the world's largest consumer of aluminum.

If Knox was neither the most celebrated nor the longest-lived mass producer of aircooled production cars, it was at least the first. Knox's initial effort was the Knox Gasoline Runabout of 1901; close on its heels was a light delivery van with basically the same running gear. The Knox van was capable of carrying three hundred pounds of cargo in addition to the driver and his supplies. It was a three-wheeler with a five-foot wheelbase and a turning circle of nine feet. Sales literature of the period claimed that the small turning circle made a reverse gear unnecessary and that the three-wheeled stance put fewer torsional stresses on the frame.

To people familiar with the internals of these vans they were affectionately known as "Old Porcupines," the result of their odd cylinder configuration. Threaded rods of three-sixteenths-inch diameter were screwed into the single horizontal cylinder. These rods took the place of the cooling fins that are more familiar to us. Knox manuals stated that their pin method made it possible "to obtain thirty-two square inches of heat radiating surface per square inch of outside surface. . . . This is about four and one half times of that obtainable with the ordinary type of aircooled cylinder with cast flanges." In aircooled engines the amount of heat carried off depends upon the total surface area exposed, the velocity and amount of cooling air, and the cylinder head and ambient temperatures.

Naturally the simplest method of aircooling is to allow the forward motion of the vehicle to carry the air flow over the exposed surface area. But this method poses one major problem, its relative inefficiency at low speeds. Accordingly, Knox installed a fan driven off the crankshaft by means of a leather belt and thus made his vehicle practical for use at the reduced speeds and stopping associated with driving around town. This was vital since heat transfer from a surface such as a cylinder head requires four times the weight of air for each degree of temperature reduction as compared to water. This means that the volume of air required to maintain thermal efficiency must be four thousand times that of water.

Apparently Knox did his homework concerning the thermal efficiency of air cooling internal combustion engines. In 1902 Knox's three entries won two of the four cups and received three first-class certificates in the New York-Boston Reliability Contest. In 1903 there was a competition held between commercial vehicles in New York City in order to demonstrate the capabilities of motorized cargo haulers before local merchants. The horse and wagon were about to take another beating, and Knox's two entries captured first and second place. While most of the watercooled entries overheated, the Knox cars

demonstrated the superiority of gasoline over steam, electricity or compressed air and thrust the gas trucks far ahead of poor Dobbin and the buckboard.

One can readily understand a consumer's concern over the reliability of an automobile's cooling system. System failures of this type do great and expensive harm to engines. Components absorb temperature rises until red heat and then seize. If an inattentive operator were to allow the engine temperature to go beyond the operational boundaries, most likely even before total engine seizure, the incoming charge of fuel would probably explode as it entered the cylinder, firing back through the carburetor.

The valve gear of the earliest Knox three-wheeled autos consisted of a single poppet valve acting as both intake and exhaust valve. An auxiliary piston valve placed the chamber in contact with the vapor supply. By 1903 the valve gear was made up of a shaft driven at half the speed of the crankshaft by spiral gears. The valve shaft actuated the exhaust valves by means of cams. The inlet valve remained a poppet-type that operated automatically by the suction or vacuum created by the downward motion of the piston. Ignition was by jump spark with fixed timing except when starting. There were eight dry cell batteries in the '01. Only four cells were used when the batteries were fully charged and four were held in reserve. Enclosed in the "igniter box" was a set of platinum points. These were to be adjusted and cleaned every five hundred miles.

Lubrication for the engine bearings was handled by a large sight feed oil cup containing sufficient lubricant for a two-hundred-mile run. Suspension was by three twenty-six-inch elliptic springs, one in the front and two in the rear. To slow the vehicle a band acted on the outer drum of the friction clutch. Factory literature boasted that the vehicle could be brought to a halt within its own length from fifteen miles an hour. The front wheel diameter was twenty-six inches and the diameter of the two rear wheels twenty-eight inches. The rims were shod with two-and-one-half-inch pneumatic tires all the way around. A Baldwin chain transmitted the power from the transmission to the rear wheels. The vehicle's top speed was somewhere between twenty-five and thirty miles per hour. The cost of all of this mechanical wizardry was $750 to $825, F.O.B. Springfield, Massachusetts. Total vehicle weight was approximately 675 pounds.

Knox offered a four-wheeler in 1902. According to *The Horseless Age* of August 10th, 1901, it was designed to "fill the gap for a strong, simple, powerful and neat appearing single seated vehicle." It could carry up to four people if the front seat was opened up. This vehicle's engine also used the pin cooling design of earlier models. It produced roughly eight horsepower, and it had an emergency brake which operated on the rear axle, independently of the foot-operated service brakes. Like other cars of the period using planetary transmissions, it could be reversed by depressing a pedal with the foot. The two forward speeds were obtained by moving the large hand-operated lever to the right or left. Like the '01 and earlier models the frame was angle steel. Some manufacturers of contemporary cars of the period, such as Franklin, used seasoned ash. The '02 had a sixty-nine-inch wheelbase and a fifty-four-inch tread. The tires were thirty by three on all four rims. The company guaranteed a top speed in excess of thirty miles per hour and the ability to climb twelve percent grades at twelve miles per hour. The entire body could be easily separated from the frame by removing four bolts, providing access to the internal mechanicals.

By 1904 gas buggies were beginning to be commonplace, so commonplace, in fact, that they were becoming the objects of theft. To protect owners a special feature is mentioned in the 1904 sales catalog, a kind of ignition key-plug. The plug was screwed into a threaded hole when the vehicle was to be started. The operator pushed the plug down into the hole to close the ignition electrical connection. To open the connection and kill the engine the operator pulled up on the plug. And to prevent unauthorized use the plug was unscrewed

*Opposite: 1901 Three-Wheeler • Owner: Wayne McKinley; Above: 1902 Runabout • Owner: Charles E. Schoettlin; Below: 1902 Runabout • Owner: Bill Kuring*

completely and slipped into the pocket. And by 1904 the regular production models of the Knox Automobile Company had twin horizontal cylinders, which were mounted low in the frame under the carriage in order to lower the center of gravity and provide a stable mobile platform.

The company's advertisements for the six styles of passenger cars and six styles of commercial vehicles offered in 1904 stressed the Knox's modernity and dependability. Their product was billed as "the car that obviates the 'tow.'" The company described its products as "the diamonds of the automobile world.... They are brilliant as diamonds in service and always at par, easy to operate, and wear like diamonds."

But promotional literature insisted that dependability was not the only virtue of the 1904 Knox; it was also beautiful. Beneath an artist's representation of the "Lenox" Touring Car, for example, was the injunction for the reader to "Note the dignified poise of the body, and that lack of 'cramped room' which predestines two-fold comfort—physical comfort and comfort to your aesthetic self-respect. The beauty of the Knox is the beauty of proportions reinforced by constructive quality of an exalted type." Beauty was even claimed to be a selling point of Knox trucks; the "Murray" Delivery Car was said to be "stately," possessing "all the earmarks of consistent architecture," while the "Davis" Delivery Car was described as being "graceful" and "charming."

By 1907 Knox automobiles featured many improvements and innovations. One for which they were most noted was their advanced clutch mechanism. This was a combination of conical surfaces, with cork inserts used in conjunction with a leather facing. These clutches were of a relatively large diameter and were housed inside the flywheel. The cones were made of aluminum with the large cork inserts staggered over their surfaces. They were brought into direct engagement with an iron ring bolted onto the flywheel, and a housing was provided to retain lubricant introduced to the friction surface by centrifugal force.

Early Knox commercial vehicles developed a reputation for reliability and power to spare. An article demonstrating the public's growing awareness of the practical applications of motorized vehicles appeared in *The Horseless Age* of January 7th, 1907 and stated in part: "A Knox aircooled 35-40 horsepower chassis was equipped some months ago as an emergency outfit for use in conjunction with the Springfield, Massachusetts fire department. The work done by this machine has been very satisfactory, as it has attended every alarm since its adoption. The attention of those interested was particularly drawn to the fact that when the auxiliary car reached the scene of the fire the driver was enabled to leave it entirely alone and assist the rest of the department; whereas in the case of the horses his entire time would be taken up in attending to them. This is one of the commercial uses to which the automobile is capable of giving efficient service."

Perhaps prompted by their marketing department and the public's view that watercooling was more conventional and efficient than was air, the Knox Company decided to offer their first watercooled auto in 1908. The Model L was basically the previous year's Model H aircooled with watercooled heads and cylinders. The method for this normally radical conversion was actually quite simple. Separate cylinder units were used, and each unit consisted of two castings, the cylinder and the head. Each cylinder had its own separate water jacket. The jacket in the casting extended almost the entire length of the cylinder wall and was enclosed at the top. Water entered at the bottom of the cylinder and exited at the top on the right-hand side.

At the upper end of the cylinder casting proper was a counter bore providing a shoulder. A ring-type asbestos gasket rested on the shoulder. The head was bolted down snugly on top of the cylinder shoulder and gasket. Water did not flow between the cylinder head and cylinder jacket. The head with its own jacket was of roughly rectangular shape and the

*Opposite and above: 1903 Delivery Van • Owner: Stanford C. Grover; Below: 1904 Flatbed Truck (before restoration) • Owner: Max Hofferbert. Following page: same 1904 truck after restoration, showing twin-cylinder porcupine design with cooling fans*

*Above: 1904 Touring Car • Owner: Harrah's Automobile Collection; Below: 1905 Runabout • Owner: Lee Hanks, Jr.; 1907 Touring Car • Owner: Kenneth B. Butler*

two-inch diameter valves sat directly in the head without removable seats. Unlike the aircooled heads, whose valves slanted at forty-five degrees in relation to the longitudinal axis of the engine, the watercooled engine's valves were within the axis.

The ease of converting from water cooling to air cooling or vice versa must have been a strong selling point. A customer could choose an identically equipped car, and depending upon his preference, have it delivered as either an aircooled or watercooled automobile. If at some point in the future he should become dissatisfied with his original choice he could have the car changed over at a reasonable cost.

Ease of maintenance was an important feature of early automobiles, since most owners repaired the vehicles themselves or had the local tinker or blacksmith work on them. The Model O was an early effort in that direction, differing from the earlier Model L in some important ways. The Model O had a slightly greater displacement, having a bore of four-and-seven-eighths inches and a stroke of four-and-three-quarters inches. It developed 38 A.L.A.M. horsepower. On the Model L the water outlet manifold was located above the heads because the water outlets of the cylinder were located in the tops of the heads. Problems arose because to remove any one head or cylinder, it was necessary to remove all the outlet connections to this manifold. To increase accessibility and thus serviceability, the cylinder outlet connections were relocated on the right side of the heads. This enabled the mechanic to remove each cylinder separately, by removing the four retaining bolts and the inlet and outlet connections of the cylinder being repaired. The single cylinder could then be removed for service.

In light of the difficulty of some of the more simple service procedures on today's European and domestic automobiles, Knox's efforts to improve serviceability are indeed remarkable. Simply changing the air conditioning belt on some foreign high performance six-cylinders requires three hands. And many home market manufacturers have stuffed their large, dated V-8 powerplants into downsized autos, frequently resulting in sparkplug access problems that provide six and seven cylinder tune-ups on eight-cylinder engines.

In addition to making maintenance easier, minor changes were made to the Knox water jackets to improve flow efficiency and eliminate any air-spaces or areas of reduced circulation. The intake manifold was relocated to the left side. Both the intake and exhaust manifold were located on the same side and were retained by the same four clamps. The single camshaft and all the pushrods remained on the right side. Model O was provided with a duplicate set of jump sparkplugs. One plug from each set was installed on either side of the head. A customer could order any standard magneto although a Spiltdorf was usually selected. The reserve battery system consisted of a "timer" on a vertical spiral gear driven shaft and a "quadruple dashboard coil with storage cells." The Model O also had a three plate clutch, while most contemporary cars still had the cone type. It had a sixteen gallon fuel tank and weighed approximately 2850 pounds.

As previously mentioned, the Knox Automobile Company made use of aluminum in their designs. The Model M had sheet aluminum fenders and the cylinders sat on an aluminum crankcase. The case sides and rear were cast as a single piece and, considering the designs of contemporary pieces, were very rigid. The front end of the case had a removable aluminum timing gear cover. The oil pan capacity was six quarts, and inside the pan was a removable strainer for larger impurities in the oil. If the timing gear cover was removed and crankshaft bearings loosened, the crankshaft could be withdrawn from the case through the cover opening.

One of the more popular commercial vehicles produced by Knox was the No. 20 Light Delivery Wagon. It was capable of carrying approximately 1500 pounds of cargo, and was powered by a ten horsepower single of the by-then famous Porcupine design. The bodywork was supported by a hot-riveted steel frame with sectional dimensions of two by

three by one-quarter inches. The wheelbase was eighty-five inches. It was suspended in the front by thirty-eight-inch semi-elliptics and in the rear by one and three-quarter-inch stock leaves forty-one inches long. The rear thirty-six and front thirty-two-inch wheels were shod with solid tires.

Braking was handled by internal expanding, *self-adjusting* shoes integral with the driven sprockets. The steering column approached the operator at a nearly vertical, bus-like angle. The delivery wagon had two speeds forward and a reverse gear carried on the end of the crankshaft like those of the larger Knox commercial vehicles. In addition to the low speed and reverse drums, a brake drum was provided with a friction band operated by a pedal. In the interest of quiet service a large Knox-designed muffler was installed. A seventeen-gallon gas tank was located under the seat, feeding a Schebler carburetor. Total vehicle weight unladen was 2505 pounds.

Nineteen-ten was the year of "The Perfect Car," if we can believe the claims of Knox Automobile Company factory sales literature. Model R was available in many different trims, but for the kingly sum of $4000 the customer could get the limousine model, complete with speaking tube and toilet case. Powered by a forty horsepower four-cylinder engine with a five-inch bore and a four-and-three-quarter-inch stroke, one motored along in one of the most luxurious automobiles then built in the United States. For persons of slightly more modest means there was a touring Model R that sold for $3250.

By 1912 Knox, like other manufacturers of the period, was building large five, six and even seven passenger touring cars, as well as two, three, and four passenger race-abouts. Harry A. Knox had long since left the company and the man responsible for design was Herman G. Farr, the head of engineering. Farr specified the use of the finest nickel alloy steels of the time. Crankshafts, camshafts, driveshafts, rear axle shafts, frames, springs and a host of other components were all made of this material.

Customers could order either the "R" or "S" powerplant. The "R" was a four-cylinder and the "S" a six. They shared the same bore and stroke of five and four-and-three-quarters inches respectively. This meant that they could share the same pistons and connecting rods. It also meant that since the cylinders were cast in pairs for strength they shared the same machinery for cylinder construction, leading to reduced tooling costs. There was also an option for a long stroke engine in both "R" and "S" form with a stroke increase from four-and-three-quarters inches to five-and-one-half inches. The "R" had five crankshaft bearings and the "S" had four. The connecting rods were drop-forged, drilled hollow for the pressure feed lubrication system. The rods had four-bolt main bearing caps.

The transmission of the '12 Knox automobiles had an aluminum case with three speeds forward and one reverse. The owner's manual claimed that once the front universal joint and clutch brake were disconnected and four retaining bolts were removed the transmission could easily be slipped from the vehicle. Control over the automobile was by the spark and throttle levers located on top of the steering wheel, the foot operated accelerator, and the clutch and brake pedals. Full floating rear axles were used on all of the closed and touring cars. On the lighter Model R autos, those carrying four passengers or fewer, including the Series C Torpedo, semi-floating rear axles were found to be sufficient.

All of the cars had contracting and expanding-type brakes. The service brake was actuated by a foot pedal which applied the outside brake band of fourteen-inch diameter and two-and-one-half-inch width. The emergency brake was an expanding type operated by adjustable eccentric cams acting on the two metal shoes lined with raybestos. The frame was of cold pressed nickel steel. Three cross members were used to link the parallel rails, one at the rear, one in the center, and one in front of the flywheel. Springs for the vehicle were made by the Bridgeport Spring Perch Company of Connecticut. Bridgeport had been

*1910 Model S Double-Rumbler Raceabout* • Owner: Eric Rosenau

*1910 Model R Touring and Details • Owner: Allan Anglemire*

making springs for wagons a hundred years before the automobile. All of the open-bodied autos were made of aluminum with a wooden base. Every sheet was hand bent and hammered. The Knox Company left customers free to choose the side of the car on which the eighteen-inch mahogany steering wheel would be installed. The wheels were artillery type with Fisk detachable rims as standard equipment and Universal rims with clincher-type tires as an option. The front axle was an I-beam type with Elliot steering yokes and Timken bearings. All models also had a "double duplex" ignition system.

The icing on the cake for most owners must have been the Knox exterior treatment. Nickel or brass plating were available as a standard feature. In fact, the Knox Company claimed that although most companies charged extra for nickel plating they did not, and that because most owners specified nickel, this type of plating was something of a Knox trademark. Painting the cars was a lovingly patient process involving four weeks and fifteen to twenty coats of paint. Customers had the option of many standard colors. Unlike Mr. Ford, who promised any color as long as it was black, Knox offered battleship gray, green, blue, royal purple, wine, maroon, carmine, tan, chocolate brown, and even a special standard color called Knox red. To satisfy even more demanding tastes there were optional shades and schemes. Knox had developed imitations of wood graining. Some of the possible selections were mahogany, rose-wood, bird's eye maple and walnut; the cost was sixty dollars. Beyond the wood grains were special combinations of standard colors in either vertical or fancy stripes which cost an additional fifty dollars.

Hand-buffed leather was used in all of the open cars, in colors best suited to match the body. Extra-fine quality leather from Mexico was also available. Closed cars were upholstered in imported goatskin, broadcloth or Bedford cord unless otherwise specified. All of the 1912 models came equipped with Bosch magnetos, Jones speedometers, Gray and Davis headlights, combination oil and electric side and taillights, shock absorbers, baggage racks, clock, foot and coat rails, pump, jack, repair kit and a full set of tools for overhaul.

Because the Knox came with so much expensive equipment, customers were free to elect not to order a fully outfitted model. Thirteen different items could be omitted, and their net cost, as well as the cost of installation and handling, deducted from the standard purchase price. Some of these items were the Jones 100 mile speedometer, $18.00; clock, $4.50; shock absorbers, $18.00; and Bosch three-field magneto, $55.00. Tops could be had in three materials: mohair, imported macintosh cloth, or pantasote, in a color to match or complement the body color. Prices for a Model S depended upon body configuration. The least expensive was the Race-about Standard at $4700 and the most expensive the Limousine Colonial seven passenger at $6400.

In 1912 the Knox Company began to experience a cash flow problem whose severity came as a surprise to many stockholders. But on October 3rd, 1912 *Motor Age* reported that "there was hardly enough cash on hand to meet the weekly payroll last week." This occurred despite the fact that orders for new vehicles were coming in daily and manufacturing's only problem was filling them fast enough. The appointed trustees, E.O. Sutton and H.G. Fisk, issued the following official statement on behalf of the stockholders: "The Knox Company's financial difficulty is due to the large purchases of material which had to be made to fulfill orders for commercial, fire and pleasure cars some types of which consumed long periods of time from the date of receipt of the order and the payment received date, and the capital of the company was not up to the strain."

The October 12th, 1912 issue of *The Horseless Age* confirmed this assessment of the situation. The trustees reported that the company's liabilities were $1,000,000 and its assets $1,250,000. Sutton and Fisk were given four months in which to accomplish their task; if they were unsuccessful and the company declared bankrupt, they were free to put the company on the auction block and convert all of the rights and property into cash. In

the meantime the plant in Springfield continued to operate and it was business as usual for the five hundred employees in their plant of 130,680 square feet.

This was not the first time the company had been in financial straits. During the Panic of 1907, in the absence of ready money and the consequent lull in sales, the firm had been forced into the hands of A.N. Mayo as assignee. At that time the liabilities were $560,000 and the assets estimated at $970,000. After being in the charge of Mayo for six months the company was reorganized.

Public demand and awareness of the marque's reliability and quality remained high, despite the company's worsening financial problems. On October 16th, 1912 *The Horseless Age* ran an article in their commercial vehicle section reporting: "There appeared in the streets of New York last week a monster vehicle which attracted as much attention as a circus parade. It was a fifteen ton capacity ash wagon drawn by a Martin tractor, one of the products of the Knox Automobile Company. The wagon is twelve feet in height and twenty-six in length, and it looks very much like a house moving down the street."

At a meeting of the stockholders of the company on October 15th, 1912, it was decided to continue the operation of the plant after the committee of stockholders which had been delegated to "investigate" conditions at the factory reported favorably. Then, on February 15th, 1913 the Knox Automobile Company was adjudged bankrupt by Judge Morton of Boston. But there was considerable difference of opinion among the five hundred creditors as to whether a liquidation of the new company or the continuance of the plan of reorganization would prove most beneficial to all concerned. It seems strange to find an excess of assets over liabilities of approximately $400,000; this could have represented considerable equity for the stockholders. One might also note that one of the largest stockholders was the estate of Alfred N. Mayo, the man who had operated as the company's president for the five years prior to his death on June 12th, 1912.

On April 15th, 1914 Charles Gardner, a trustee of the Knox Automobile Company, valued the company at $1,634,414.89. It was announced that the company would be auctioned off on the steps of the Hampden County Court House. A short account of the proceedings appeared in *The Horseless Age* of April 29th, 1914: "Objections on the part of an attorney for the majority of the stockholders, who claimed invalid proceedings in bankruptcy, did not halt the auction sale of the bankrupt Knox Automobile Company . . . but the low bid offered by the sole bidder for the plant had the desired effect. . . . Although the court had appraised the value of the plant in excess of $1,600,000.00 the best, and incidentally the only bid was for $350,000.00. . . . This bid was made by E.O. Sutton who claimed that he was bidding as an individual, but admitted that the heirs of A.N. Mayo, former president of the company, were interested."

On May 1st, 1914, Sutton increased the bid to $631,090 and the referee in bankruptcy, Charles W. Bosworth, approved the sale. John P. Wright of Boston, the attorney representing "a majority of the stockholders," tried to stop the sale by questioning the legality of the entire bankruptcy. At the hearing before the referee it was disclosed that the sale of the plant to Sutton would result in a loss of $900,000 over the appraised value of the property.

Circumstances surrounding the end of the company called Knox have been somewhat obscured by time. The name of the company became The Knox Motors Company after the sale, and the best sources indicate that there was a short-lived merger between Knox Motors and the Militor Corporation. (See AUTOMOBILE *Quarterly*, Volume XIX, Number 4). If there is anything to be learned from following these financial gymnastics, it is this: technical virtuosity, innovation, product versatility and even high sales did not always insure the stability of early automobile companies. If they had, names like Marmon, Franklin and Knox might be as familiar today as Ford, Chevrolet and Chrysler.

*1914 Knox-Martin Tricycle Tractor • Owner: San Jose Fire Department*

F-D 4 Place Cabin Speedster

# The Career and the Creations of Alan H. Leamy

By Dan Burger

Of those who have admired or even acquired examples of the automotive design of Alan H. Leamy, only a few would associate his name with the automobiles he styled. Today museums and collectors of fine automobiles place his creations among their most highly regarded possessions. Although Leamy himself has remained nearly unknown, authorities agree that the work of this self-taught stylist captured the essence of what has been called the Golden Age of the automobile.

His designs, executed during a period of less than ten years, were among the most noteworthy creations of the American automobile industry. His peers had enormous regard for his artistic abilities. The products of these skills captured the imagination of the general public. Leamy's work had a distinct quality that makes an immediate impact and commands instant recognition. Fortunately, he was employed for most of his career by the uninhibited Errett Lobban Cord. Leamy would offer much of the inspiration in Cord's quest to provide "more than mere transportation."

Alan H. Leamy was born on June 4th, 1902 in Arlington, Maryland. At the time of his birth his father, also named Alan Leamy, worked in Baltimore as an employee of the Welsbach Company of Philadelphia, a manufacturer of gas mantles. But when the child was three the family moved to Columbus, Ohio, where the elder Leamy served as Welsbach's district manager.

At about that time young Alan contracted polio, resulting in the permanent impairment of his left leg. During his adult years Leamy depended for mobility on a leg brace and cane, and compensated for his handicap by dressing impeccably, with conservative elegance. He loved fast driving, and learned to use his arm to lift his leg onto the clutch so quickly and deftly that some of his passengers were unaware of the procedure. Despite his disability he became an enthusiastic hunter. Eventually he built up a respectable gun collection and worked on designs for experimental bullets and gun stocks.

Although Leamy may have been endowed with natural artistic aptitude, those who knew him during his childhood claimed that his handicap became an incentive for sharpening his powers of observation and concentration, intellectual ability and zeal for achievement. He had drawn cars since his earliest boyhood, and later took a correspondence course in architecture. As a young man he showed his bride the group of row houses in Atlantic City that he had designed. Later, while working in Auburn, he attended anatomy classes in Fort Wayne. Although he did not pursue his full-time education beyond high school, Leamy read widely in the fields of music, literature, science and medicine, and older acquaintances found him an engaging and remarkably well informed conversationalist.

In 1925, when he was 23, Alan Leamy married Agnes Garrett of Swarthmore, Pennsylvania, daughter of Sylvester Garrett, founder of Philadelphia's Garrett-Buchanan Paper Company. The prospect of a disabled, self-educated in-law who was as yet uncommitted to a profession was unappealing to the family. During this period Leamy was unhappily occupied in selling real estate for the financially unstable Samuel Bader Agency of Ventnor, New Jersey, and devoting much of his leisure time to making sketches of automobiles.

Sympathizing with his son's love of cars and evident artistic talent, Leamy's father then wrote to Thomas Litle, Jr., a former colleague at Welsbach, who had gone on to become chief engineer at the Marmon Motor Company in Indianapolis. Litle's response to the elder Leamy's recommendation of his son was both gracious and generous. "I am only too glad," he wrote, "to champion the cause of a boy who is just starting out, and who has, I believe, considerable ability and I will watch him as closely as I would my own son and try to advise him accordingly." Thus Leamy's eighteen-month career as a real estate salesman came to an end and his automotive career was launched.

Alan Leamy worked at Marmon under the tutelage of Litle between March 1927 and April 1928. Gradually he became dissatisfied there. Mrs. Leamy recalls that Alan was an admirer of the designs of such European manufacturers as Hispano-Suiza and Isotta-Fraschini. "He felt American cars were too conservative, too far behind the design and engineering features of the foreign cars." As an admirer of

Alan Leamy in his office on the second floor of Auburn Automobile Company's Administration Building. The range of his interests was wide, as is shown by the designs to the right: an improved bullet, a proposed mascot, and two drawings for Marmon: a Marmon 78 Four-Passenger Sport Touring Car from May 16th, 1928 and a new grille interpretation from May 6th, 1927.

the lighter colors—especially the pastels—favored by European coachbuilders and as one fascinated by the experimental front wheel drive cars of the period, Leamy found the prevailing philosophy at Marmon staid and restrictive; he was eager for a more promising opportunity to develop his personal theories about automotive design.

Based as he was in Indianapolis, Leamy learned of E. L. Cord's intention of manufacturing a front wheel drive automobile, and wrote to him in the hope of obtaining a position. Cord referred the letter to the chief of the front wheel drive project, Cornelius Willett Van Ranst. In April 1928 Van Ranst directed Leamy to meet with him at the Duesenberg factory in Indianapolis, site of the restricted-entry section in which the front wheel drive project was underway. Van Ranst was so impressed with the sketches Leamy showed him that he passed them to Cord, whose response was equally favorable. Thus, in August 1928, the young man assumed the enviable position of chief stylist for America's first front wheel drive production car.

At Auburn Leamy found himself among a select group of consultants and staff members who included some of the pioneers of American front wheel drive technology. Harry Miller, from whom the basic front wheel drive layout was obtained, lent his expertise as a consultant. Cornelius Van Ranst coordinated the joint efforts of Leon Duray, Leo Goossen and Harry Miller to translate Miller's racing car designs into a viable passenger car concept, and to integrate this concept with Auburn motor and transmission components. Chief engineer Herb Snow and body designer John Oswald were two other important co-workers.

Since Auburn was a small manufacturer, Leamy had major responsibility for the design of the new car's interior and exterior. This gave him the opportunity to actualize his theory that the successful car must be designed as a unit. Given an environment conducive to fresh thinking and experimentation, Leamy made changes that dramatically altered the products of the Auburn Automobile Company. These innovations would be absorbed by the American and European automotive industries.

In Leamy's execution of the L-29 Cord body design, new conceptions of styling were introduced. Because of the front wheel drive factor and the lowness that allowed, Leamy enjoyed the luxury of a chassis that would permit his design to attain its maximum effectiveness. The L-29 Cord was, indeed, the unified creation that Leamy had desired. While the front wheel drive mechanism was acclaimed for its technological advancement, the L-29's exterior design caused as great a sensation throughout the automotive world, and received equally enthusiastic coverage in the international press.

Strother MacMinn, noted educator in the field of automotive design at the Art Center College, Pasadena, a designer with informed insight into the classics, describes Leamy's work as "artful interpretation." "Al Leamy was an extraordinarily talented designer," says MacMinn. "The exaggerations that he was able to include in the design of the radiator, the flair of the fenders, and the placement of the elements on the front of the car, for example, were masterpieces in discretion and proportion." Notable among the car's design attributes is the appearance of unity reflected in meticulous detail. Even the dust shield, which covers the fuel tank and frame, is embossed with the design that is also prominent on the radiator and fenders.

Some typed notes that Leamy prepared for an interview at the time of the L-29's introduction reflect the stylist's thoughts on automobile design. His philosophy transcended the traditional practice of making the body fit the chassis, as the following excerpt suggests. "Body designs have been influenced to a great extent by the horse drawn vehicle it replaced. Body designing was often an afterthought. The changes, from year to year, were most often the result of some change or improvement in the chassis itself. The engineering departments were usually responsible for making these changes and made them as well appearing as possible. If the result was pleasing to the public eye and especially to women, the sales value was immediately apparent. Time and again, we have seen a change in design in a certain car followed by public acceptance and this feature of design would soon be copied by other manufacturers.

"Mr. E. L. Cord was one of the first executives to sense and foresee the sales possibilities of artistically designed

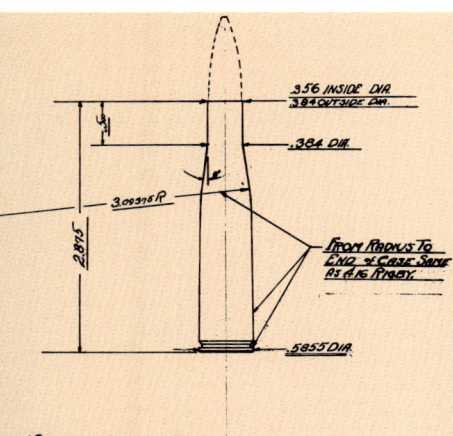
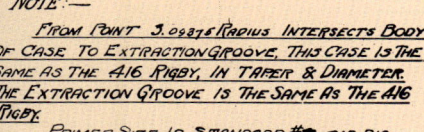

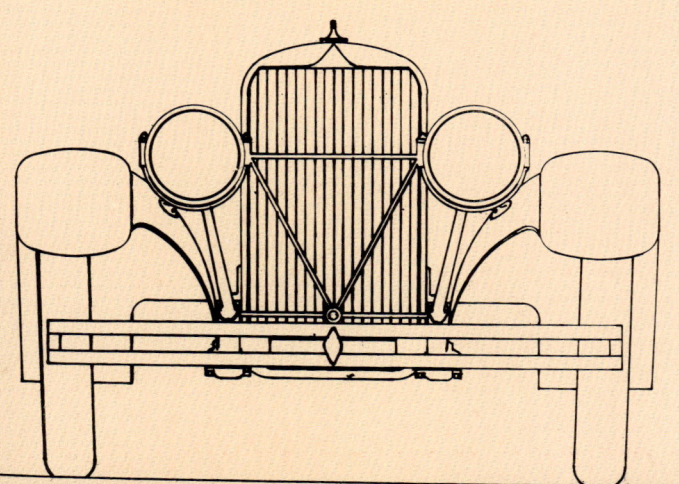

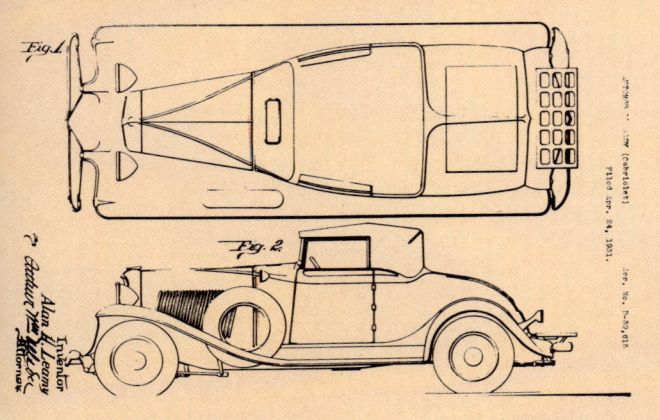

Above: two of Leamy's patent drawings, for the Auburn Cabriolet submitted on April 24th, 1931 (left) and for the front-drive L-29 Cord submitted on June 24th, 1929. In corresponding with the Employment Service of the Society of Automotive Engineers on September 28th, 1933, he summarized his accomplishments. "The complete exterior design of the Cord Front Drive was entirely mine. Following the Cord, I designed the 8-98 model, and subsequent models of the Auburn.... I have designed the building of quite a few Custom and Experimental models on Cord and Auburn chassis. Previous to my association with Auburn I was with the Marmon Motor Company, and designed their last series of large eights."

Three views of a wooden mockup produced from one of Leamy's designs by the Experimental Department of Auburn in about 1931. Design was never used in an actual car.

automobiles and instead of depending upon the engineering force for designing the body for the new Cord front drive, he created a special department upon whom the responsibility for the appearance of the car would depend."

In his capacity as chief stylist, Leamy was also responsible for the Auburn automobile line. Recognition of the marque was increasing, basically as a result of E. L. Cord's successes with the straight eight engine and colorful paint schemes. Leamy's first assignment was to update the well-established Auburn sedan, giving it bigger doors and other features to increase passenger comfort. E. L. Cord's desire to see the effect of the changes on a full-sized car led to what was apparently Auburn's first project involving large scale clay models.

While it is extremely unlikely that Leamy had previous experience with clay modeling, draftsman A. E. Williams, who worked on the front wheel drive project, recalled that Leamy instructed him and a group of pattern makers in constructing a clay model 1929 Auburn sedan during the fall and winter of 1928. "The pattern makers built a 'dummy' body to the approximate shape of the Auburn sedan body. We'd plaster it with clay," Williams recounted, "and mold it from templates taken off the actual full-size body drawings that Leamy and Oswald would have done." Using paddles, trowels and sculpting tools, the model was shaped to the exact contours. "Al taught us the tricks of the trade. We made our tools out of heavy wire which was ground to fine cutting edges. Without his expertise, we wouldn't have gotten to first base." The model was completely detailed. Wheels were placed in position, glass was inserted into window recesses and it was painted and striped. "You would swear it was an actual car," observes Williams, referring to photographs taken at the time.

During this same period Leamy rendered a series of Duesenberg models. While it is not documented, there are strong indications that Al Leamy influenced the development of the famed Model J. Comparison of the Duesenberg to the L-29 reveals the Leamy line. Designer Strother MacMinn draws attention to the elements peculiar to Leamy's characteristic style. He questions whether there were any others present at that time who possessed the sensitivity to create those beautiful Duesenberg radiator shells which are "completely unique and probably the noblest things that ever happened on the classic American automotive scene."

MacMinn points out the use of a wide shoulder at the top of the radiator shell. The form gracefully tapers downward as it continues outward, suggesting a gently rounded heart. Through the use of this radiator design, Leamy created a unique identity, and an artistic focal point

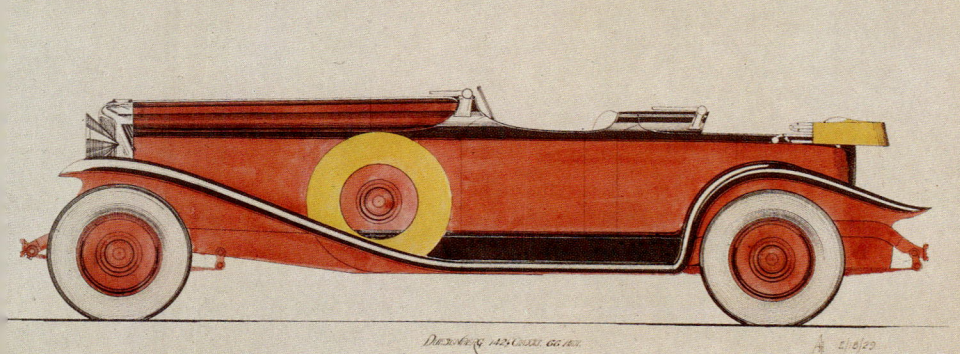

Color drawings on this and following pages show the evolution of Leamy's designs between March of 1928 and October of 1929.

This page: a firm believer in life-size and scale-model clays, Leamy supervised the creation of these Experimental Department models for the 1934 Auburn. Opposite: views of a plaster scale model developed in the Experimental Department for a proposed 1934 Auburn that was not built.

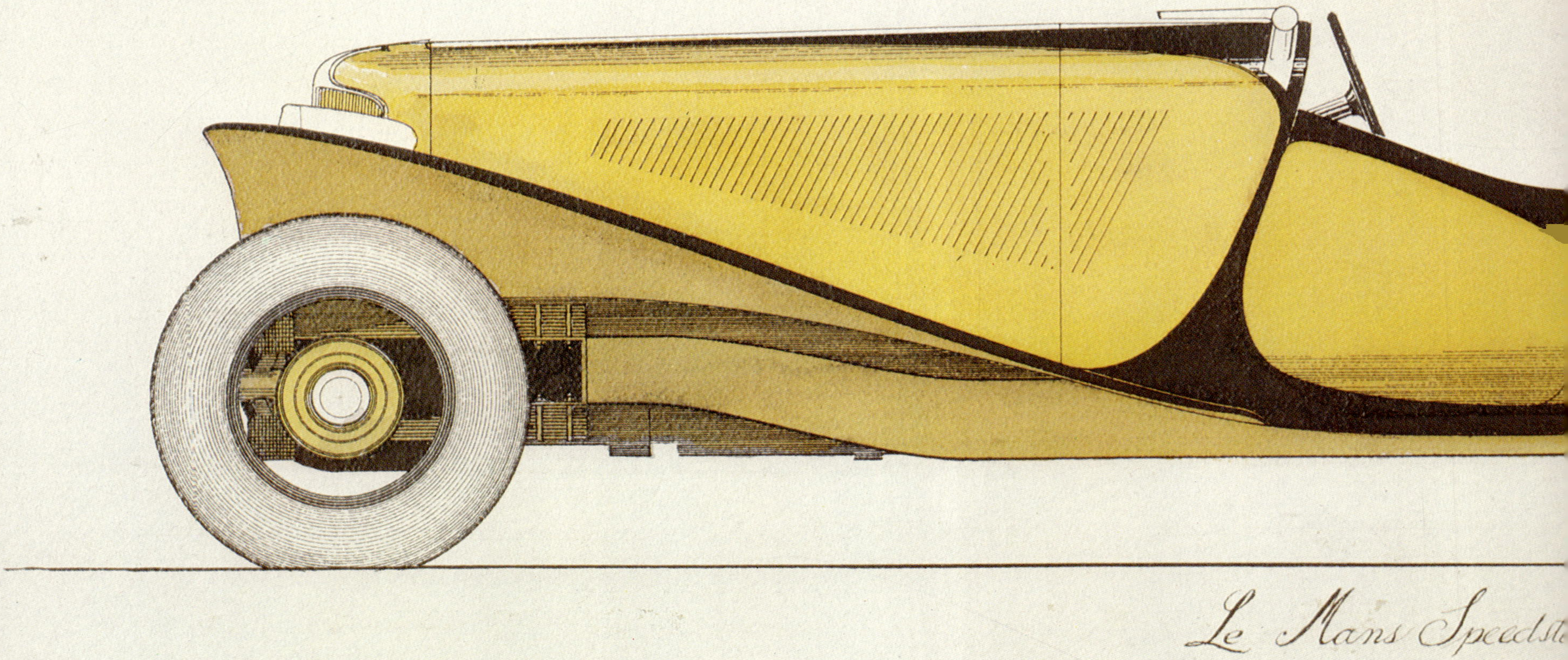

Le Mans Speedster

that blended with the entire body form, including the hood. Also illustrative of Leamy's technique is the interpretation of the clamshell fender. Beginning with a convex arch over the front wheel, the arch form is continued, almost endlessly, until finally reversing into the running board. MacMinn describes it as a "marvelous, long, leaping flair. Nobody did this quite like Leamy did." His work demonstrated a unification of form and proportion that had not yet been expressed in the mechanically oriented automotive field.

The question of Leamy's contribution to the Duesenberg design was also commented on by Duesenberg designer Herb Newport, who saw the resemblance to the L-29 and the fact that both cars were introduced almost simultaneously as evidence suggesting Leamy's involvement. Because the front wheel drive project was underway at the Duesenberg factory until August of 1928, when Leamy was present, it seems likely that Leamy's fresh ideas gained acceptance within the Model J program. Somewhat later, when designer Gordon Buehrig came to the Duesenberg program, he remarked that the radiator and fender line already established was too perfect for him to tamper with.

The 8-98 Auburn, introduced in 1931, was the first production line Auburn to which Al Leamy fully devoted his considerable talents. It would become, in the midst of the Depression, the best selling Auburn of all time. In contrast to the emphasis which exaggerated the distinctively low profile of the L-29 Cord, Leamy used the high body and frame of the Auburn chassis and engine to an equally dramatic effect. Auburn's reputation for performance had been extended at that time thanks to a number of national speed and endurance records. At the beginning of the new Auburn design program Leamy conferred frequently with those involved in the company's high speed performance testing, and he modified his proposals and designs on the basis of what he learned from them.

To dramatize the powerful Lycoming Straight Eight engine, Leamy's design made use of the naturally long, high hood. The car's overall appearance announced the presence of high performance. Focal point of this vertical design theme was another master presentation of individualism— the radiator shell. In keeping with the corporate image present in both Cord and Duesenberg, Leamy began with the high-shoulder appearance. In achieving a unique identity for the Auburn, MacMinn notes that Leamy's use of the center split was "the key to a fresh, modern look. The Auburn radiator design visually suggests a hole into which air would naturally flow." Capitalizing on this identifiable design feature, once again Leamy had hit the mark of a

139

Three pencil drawings from the latter period of Leamy's career. Idea for Packard front-drive sedan done on April 25th, 1933, during the period when Leamy hoped to follow his mentor Cornelius Van Ranst to Packard. Packard president Alvan Macauley found his designs "too extreme." Center and right: undated views of a front-drive sedan probably executed for a prospective LaSalle or Cadillac shortly before he went to work at Fisher.

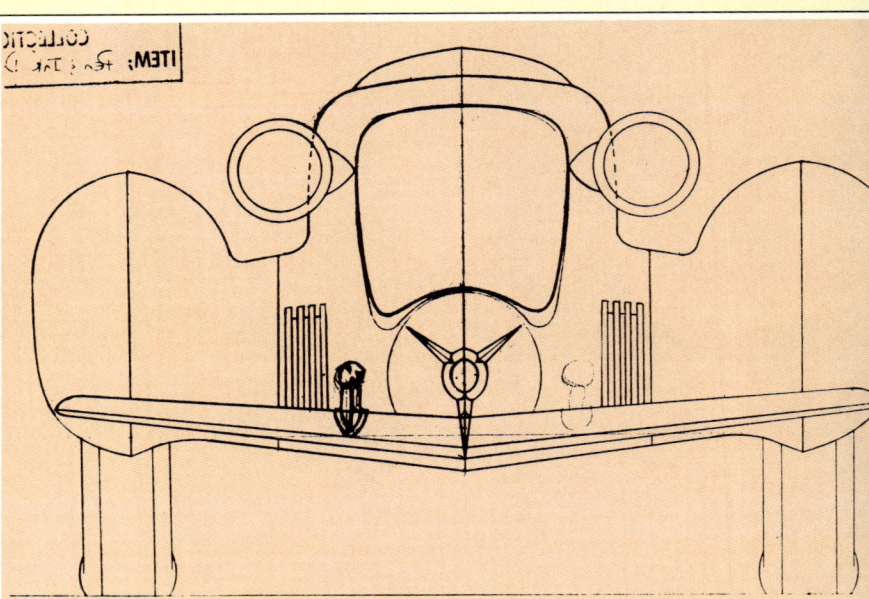

Cord Sport Phaeton

truly unique, yet totally natural form.

While the radiator and hood command attention, their importance in Leamy's styling scheme lies within the completeness of the automobile's design. Again, his concept of proportion distinguishes his work from other designs. The Auburn convertible sedan epitomizes the qualities inherent in this development of styling. Narrow windows increase the impression of overall length. The flair of the fender connotes speed. There is the characteristic attention to detail.

In the fall of 1931, Auburn added a speedster to the 8-98 series. The development of this automobile gave Leamy the opportunity to exhibit even more of his convictions about design. The raked windshield and boattail epitomize the sensation of speed, and the boattail speedster became the most enduring symbol of Auburn's popularity.

Only minor styling changes were made as the 8-98 became the 8-100 for 1932. However, in a move to position Auburn in the forefront of the affordable high performance, luxury car field, the company introduced the V-12. With essentially the same styling features as the eight cylinder Auburns, the twelves gained an extra eight inches in length by the elongation of the hood and running board area. Although the big Auburns brought stylish luxury and high performance to a more moderate price range, the new car market was now severely crippled by the nation's economy, and its effects on the Auburn Automobile Company became disabling. As the time approached for a new Auburn design in 1934, the state of the company's health demanded an austere engineering budget. As the decline in Auburn sales reached alarmingly low levels, the company laid off large numbers of employees. A subsidiary company, Limousine Body of Kalamazoo, Michigan, was closed, and production at the Auburn factories was greatly reduced.

During his first years with Cord, Leamy had enjoyed stimulating professional contacts, the opportunity to develop some of the most exciting production cars of the period, and even the chance to create a few custom-bodied automobiles. But in the present gloomy atmosphere, with the prospect of no new design responsibilities for the foreseeable future, Alan Leamy became restless. In the hope of securing a more satisfying position he made sketches of various automotive interiors and exteriors and sent inquiries to several manufacturers, including Graham and Packard, the company which his former mentor Cornelius Van Ranst had joined in 1929. Drawings forming part of Leamy's front wheel drive proposal for Packard still survive.

For a time it looked as if the new challenge that Leamy was seeking might come through his friend Alfred Ney and

141

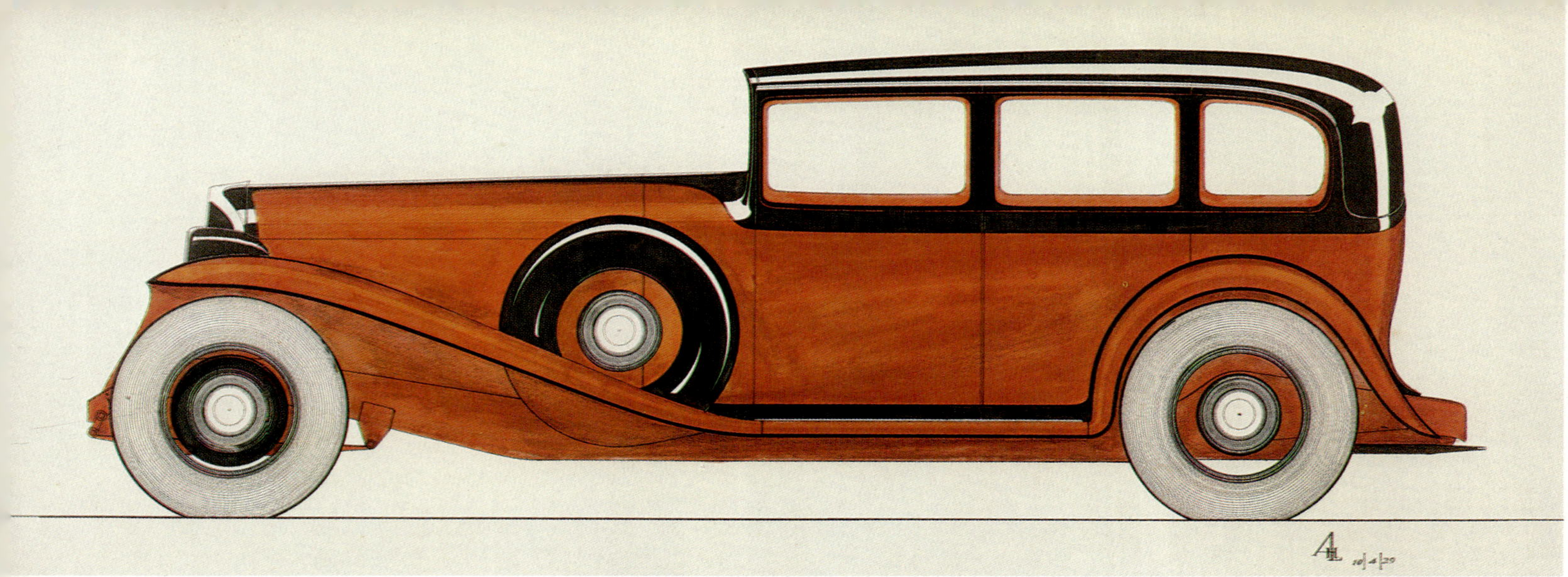
10|4|29

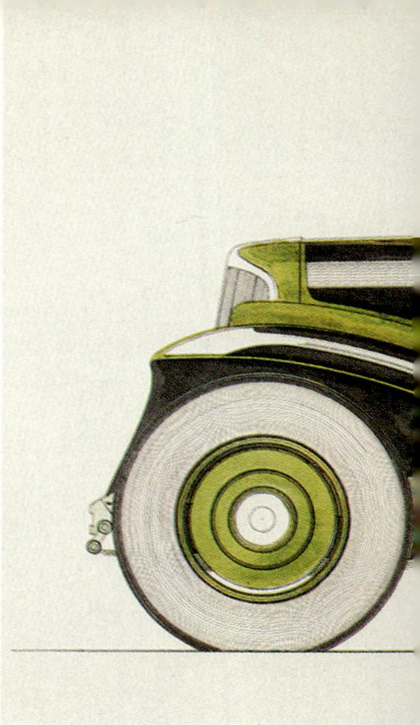

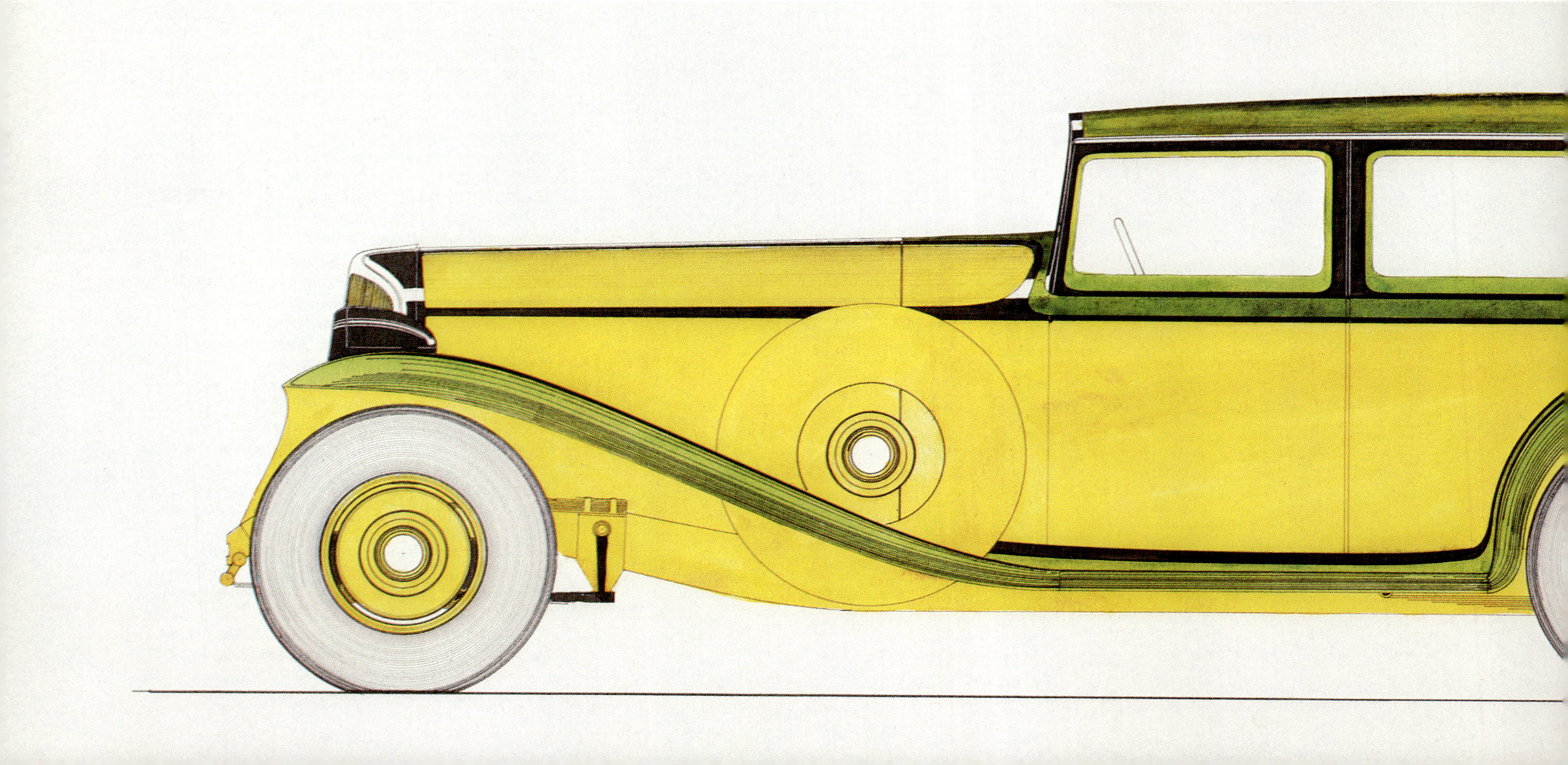

Near the end of his career Al Leamy worked on these drawings as part of a design proposal prepared for Graham.

the Bendix Company. Ney had left France and his position as an engineer with Delage in the hope of obtaining broader experience in the United States. After a period of employment at Pratt-Whitney he joined Packard's aviation department. Following that he took an engineering job at Bragg Kliesrath.

Then the Bendix Company acquired Kliesrath and Mr. Kliesrath became vice president of Bendix, whose overt business was the production of auto parts. Soon afterwards Alfred Ney learned that it was president Vincent Bendix's secret ambition to build a complete automobile that would bear his own name. Bendix set up a special division, the Steel Wheel Corporation, to create the car; only a few of his intimates knew the real nature of the company.

Ney, believing that the new car should be a front wheel drive vehicle, enlisted the assistance of Leamy, whose design expertise he had come to admire. In the small shop that Bendix provided, Ney created the car's monocoque framework, an innovative structure which had its origins in the aviation industry. Made of a precursor of bonded "Duramold" plywood, the entire frame weighed no more than 1600 pounds. Ney also created a four wheel, independent suspension system for the car. According to the design proposal, it was designed to carry five passengers, three in front and two in the rear.

Albert Ney recalls that when the chassis was completed Vincent Bendix's glee was almost childlike; as company executives and the car's creators watched, the president broke a bottle of champagne against the framework. Bendix was so eager that the car bearing his name go forth into the world that he insisted that one of the standard, heavy, wood and metal bodies of the day be attached to its frame immediately. But the delicate engine and suspension could not sustain so great a weight, and the Bendix's debut in Europe was not a triumphal progress, but a series of humiliating breakdowns in England, France and Italy.

Leamy never had the chance to create the projected body; at about this time General Motors purchased Bendix and Vincent Bendix had to turn his back on his namesake. Only the Ney-Bendix prototype was produced; it has survived to the present day.

Meanwhile, Auburn's future grew increasingly dark and Leamy continued to search for suitable new opportunities. In the summer of 1934 he found the chance he had been seeking and left Auburn to work as a designer at the Fisher Body Company. Then, a year later, Leamy was promoted to chief stylist of the LaSalle Division of General Motors. Mrs. Leamy recalls the enormous satisfaction that her husband derived during this period from Harley Earl's admiration for his work.

Leamy's friend Al Ney remembers planning a visit to Detroit to celebrate his promotion. But just before he was to leave he received a telegram containing the tragic news that Alan had suddenly died as the result of accidental septicemia from an injection medically administered.

The automotive career of Alan H. Leamy had passed in just eight years. Although only thirty-three at the time of his death, he had become instrumental in developing new trends in automobile design. His personal life has become overshadowed by the magnitude of his accomplishments— a case of performance taking precedence over presence. ✣

# L-29 CORD CABRIOLET

by
Alan H. Leamy

A COLOR PORTFOLIO

Owned by Jack Bowshier
Photographed by Roy Query

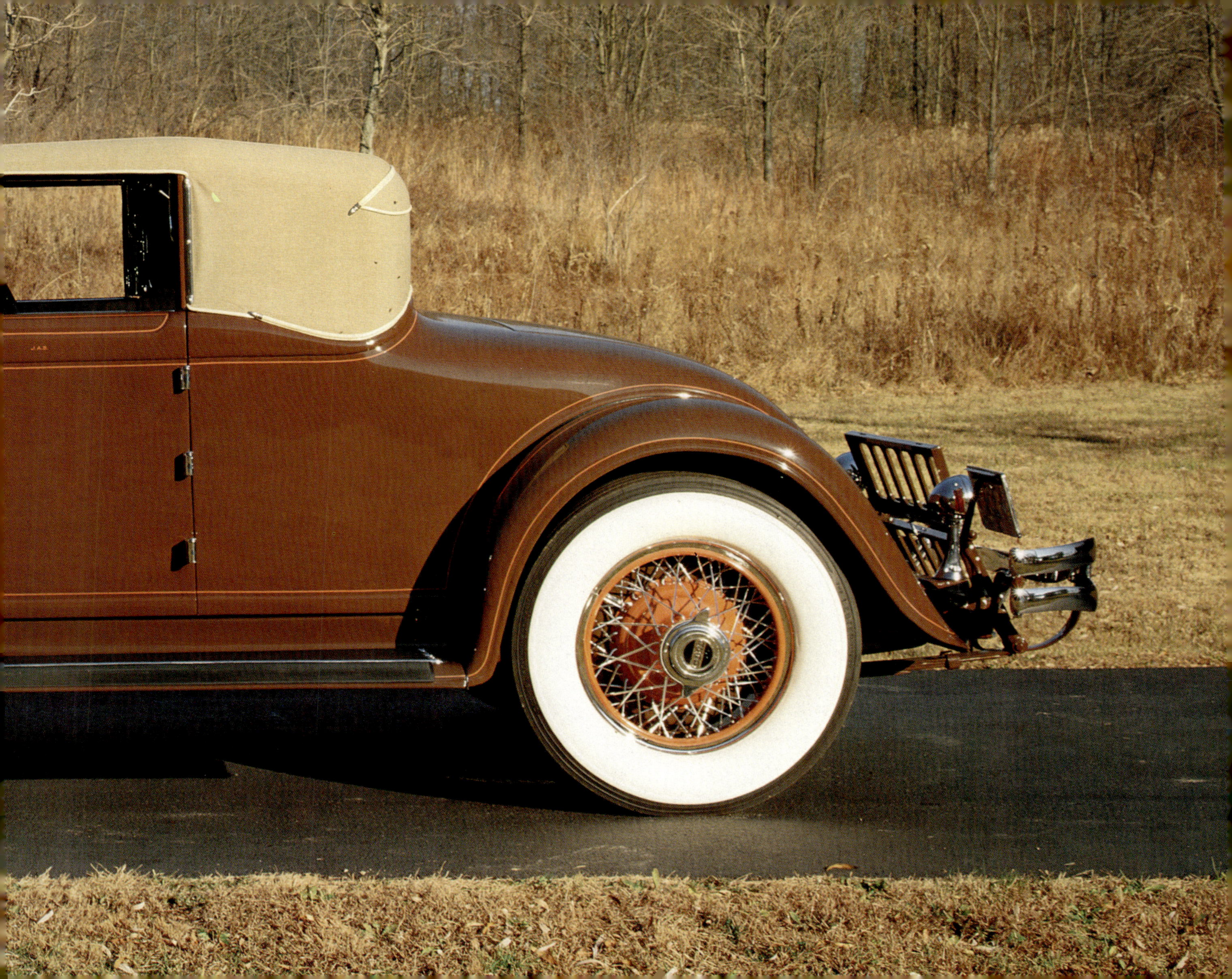

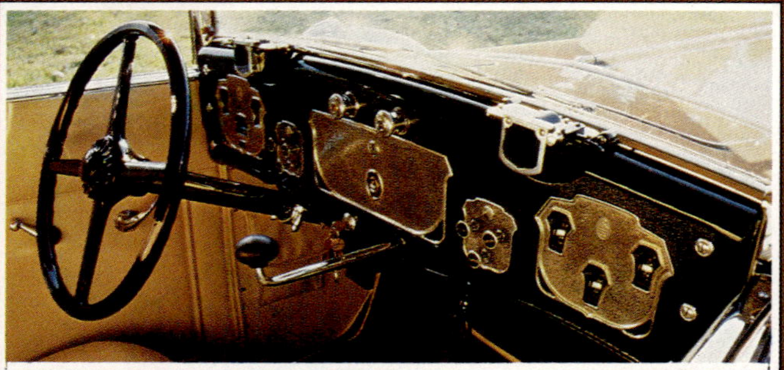
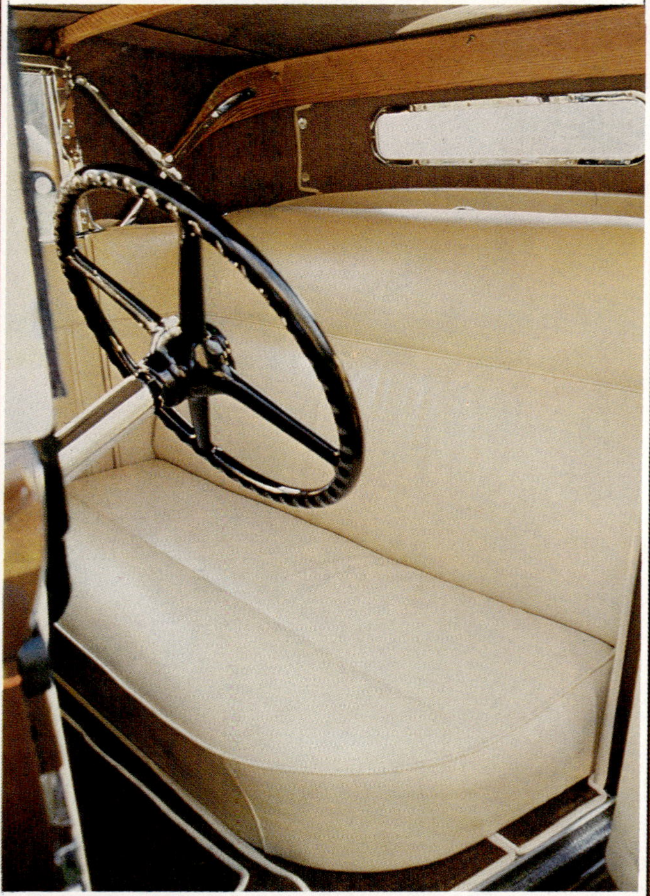
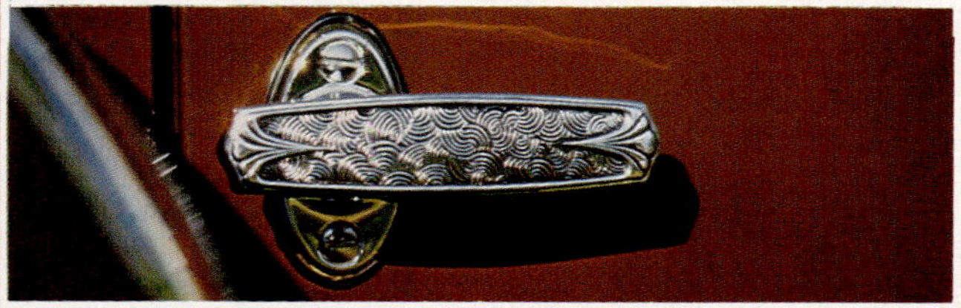
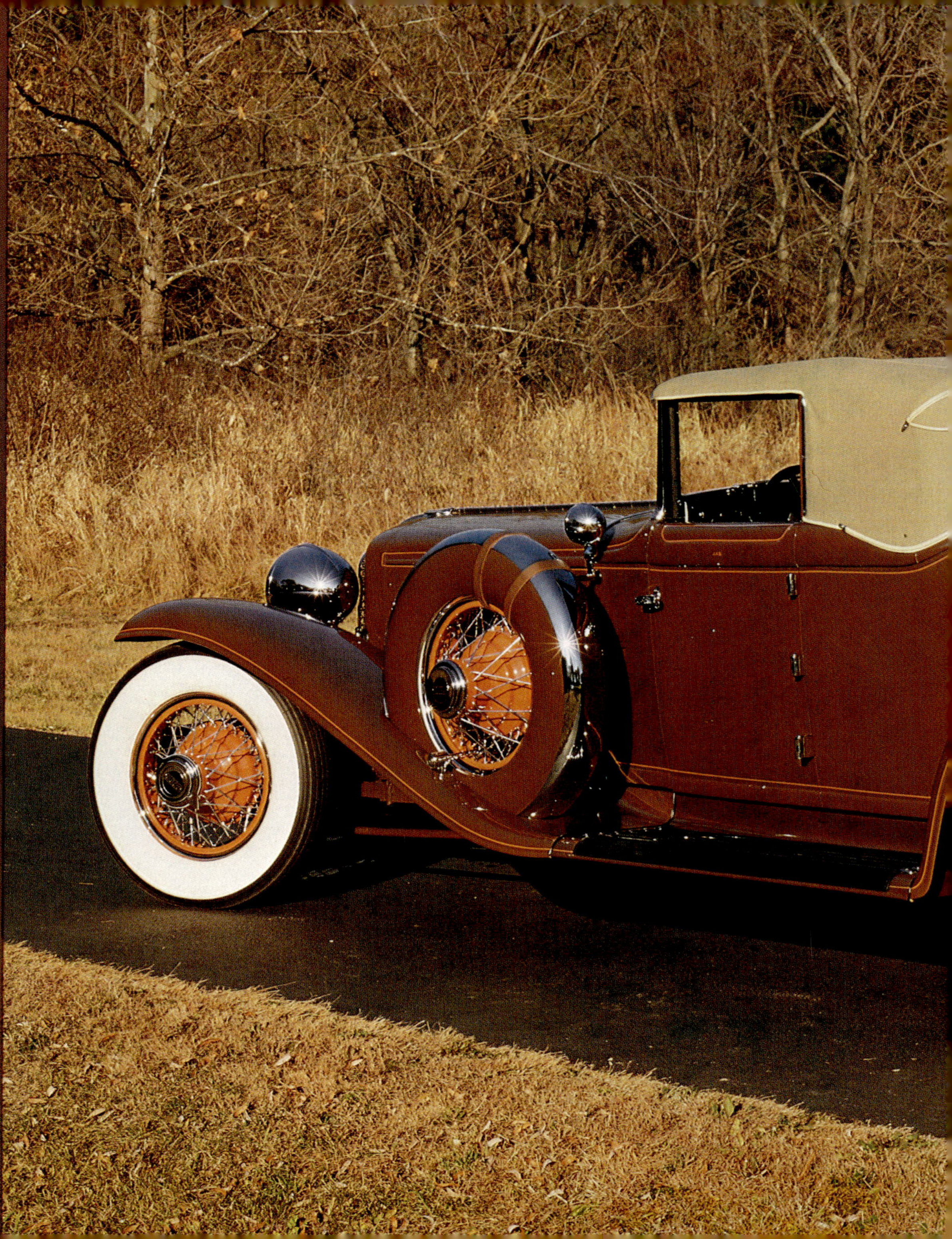

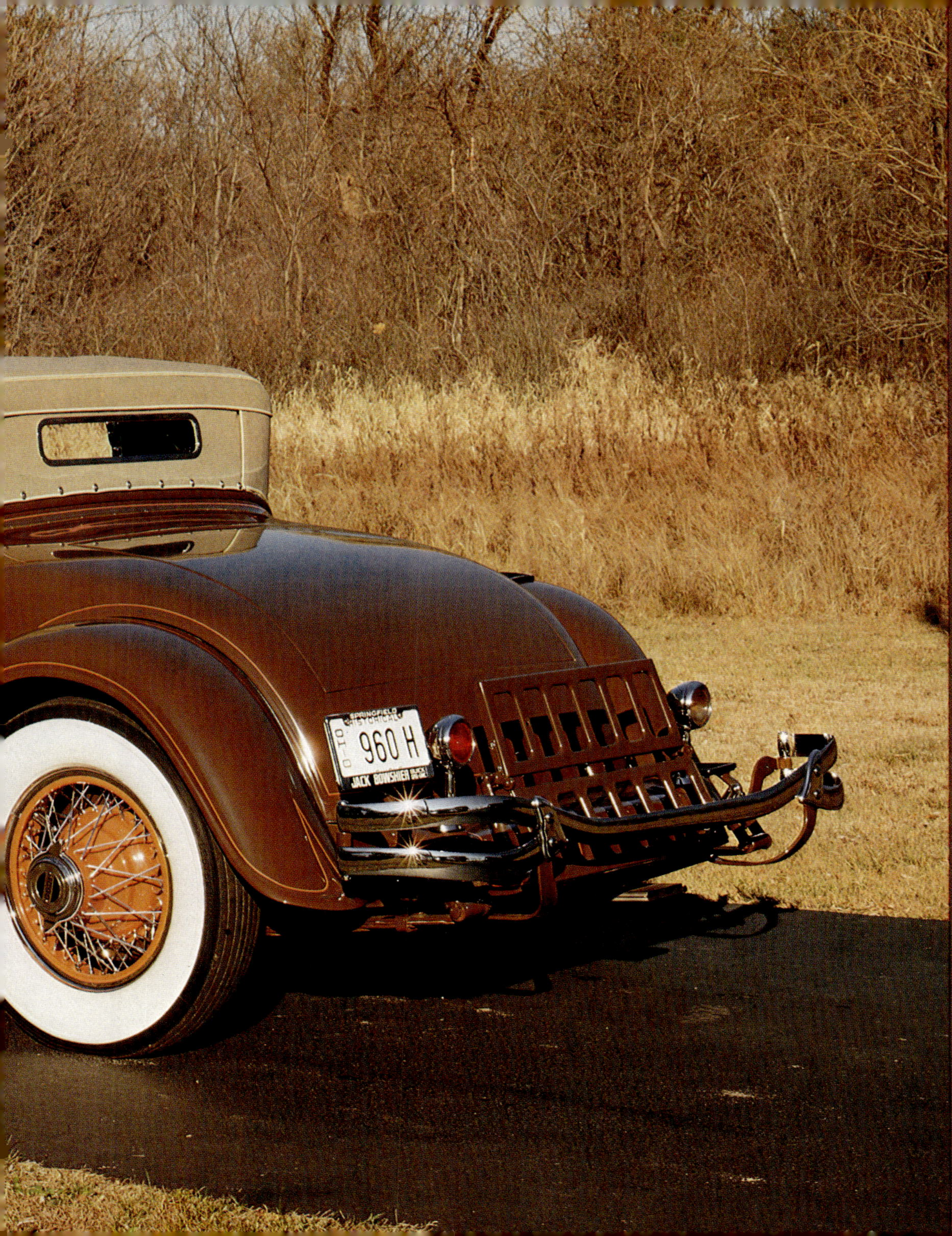
SPRINGFIELD
960 H
JACK BOWSHIER

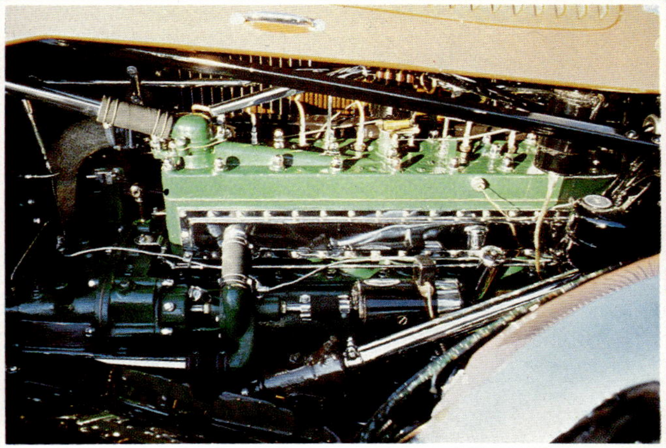

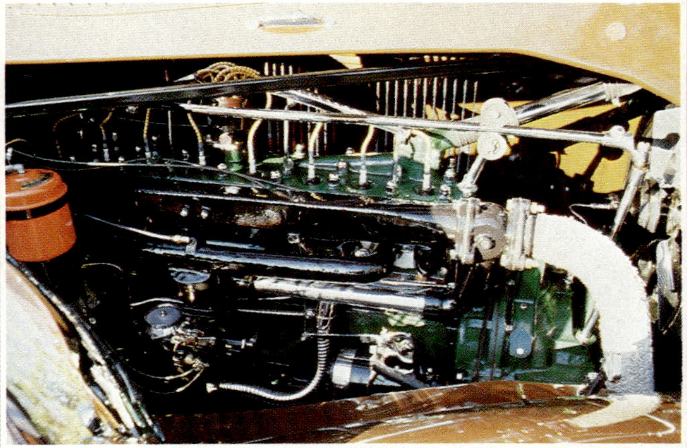

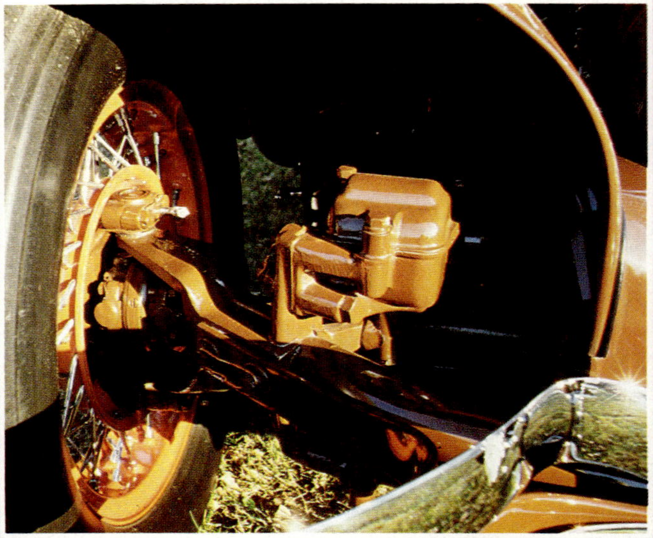

"A GENUINE LOWNESS INGE

IOUSLY ATTAINED": RUXTON

By Tom Meredith • Photography by Rick Lenz

In an era of rear-drive vehicles, the L-29 Cord did have a front-drive rival, although it was produced for such a brief time and in such small numbers that it is all but forgotten today. This was the Ruxton, marketed by Wall Street financier and promoter Archie Andrews and his New Era Motors, Incorporated. Jeff Godshall has argued that "both cars were products of the philosophy that a different car is a better car," and has compared the two automobiles.

He points out that the L-29, which sold for $3095, was a more stylish, larger, more powerful car with a longer wheelbase than the Ruxton, which cost one hundred dollars more. Design of both models was hampered by lack of development money, leading to the use, whenever feasible, of existing powerplants and related parts. Since no Ruxton road tests are extant, it is impossible to compare actual road performance, but the Ruxton was the more sophisticated car in terms of design. (See AUTOMOBILE Quarterly, Volume VIII, Number 2.)

The experimental prototype of the Ruxton was conceived in the early Twenties by William J. Muller, a development engineer with the Budd Manufacturing Company of Philadelphia, and completed at Budd during the fall of 1928. Then, on August 1st, 1929, the production prototype itself was completed. The mechanical design formulated by Muller and his associate, Colonel Ragsdale, was extremely inventive. The engine itself was a Continental Model 18S L-head straight-eight. Bore and stroke were 3.0 x 4.75 inches, with a displacement of 268.8 cubic inches. The engine developed 100 hp at 3400 rpm.

Muller's transmission was the crucial factor in Ruxton's technical success. It became clear in the course of prototype testing that the engine would have to be moved forward in the chassis if there was to be sufficient weight over the front wheels, and also clear that the eight-in-line engine would leave little room for a conventional transmission. Eager to avoid producing a car whose hood extended far forward of the cowl, Muller split the gearbox, putting low and reverse in front of the differential and second and third behind it. A unique worm gear and wheel took the place of the more traditional ring gear and pinion.

The body design of the Ruxton prototype, a four-door sedan, was equally distinctive. Executed by Budd designer Joseph Ledwinka, the Ruxton had a wheelbase of 130 inches, with tires 31 inches in diameter. But the obviously unique design feature of the Ruxton was its height. With a ten-inch ground clearance, it stood only 63.25 inches high, or ten inches lower than its rear-drive contemporaries, which offered less ground clearance. The car's front wheel drive mechanism allowed the body to be so lowered on its chassis that the hood was nearly as low as the front fenders. The lowness of the car led to the elimination of running boards, necessitating leather guards on all fenders to protect the body from scratches and splashes. Powerful, unconventionally shaped Woodlite headlamps contributed to the Ruxton's unusual appearance.

While Ruxton sedan bodies were built by Budd with stampings done from Budd dies by the Pressed Steel Company of England, roadster and town car coachwork was executed by the Baker-Raulang Company of Cleveland. Chassis manufacture was a more complicated affair, thanks to the economic dislocations of the day and the abrasive entrepreneurial style of company president Archie Andrews. By 1931 the Ruxton's short life was over. In the two years prior to its demise, the car's fortunes had become involved, usually with detrimental effect to the sponsoring firm, with no less than eight automobile companies: Hupp, Peerless, Marmon, Jordan, Stutz, Gardner, Moon and Kissel.

Despite the Ruxton's short career and limited production—hardly more than three hundred automobiles were manufactured—the Ruxton was an excellent car. And the way in which it was marketed to the public verged on the brilliant.

Andrews and his advisors quickly fixed upon the idea that Ruxton's lowness should be its chief selling point. Its lowness could be made into a symbol of technical sophistication, uniqueness and modernity. "A car so low that you can look over it.... A car so smart none can overlook it" was the slogan featured in advertisements appearing within the most glamorous magazines of the day.

The masterpiece of Ruxton advertising was a McGinnis-Aldus four-page ensemble that was published in Fortune in 1929. An Art Deco design that featured bold panels of blue, green, pink and maroon, the copy tried to convince its readers that the Ruxton was the fulfillment of all the claims they had heard made about other automobiles. "In all the vocabulary of motordom," it asserted, "there are no new nouns or verbs or adjectives to describe this new car.... So the old words, which find a new meaning, a truer definition in the Ruxton, must suffice though they have

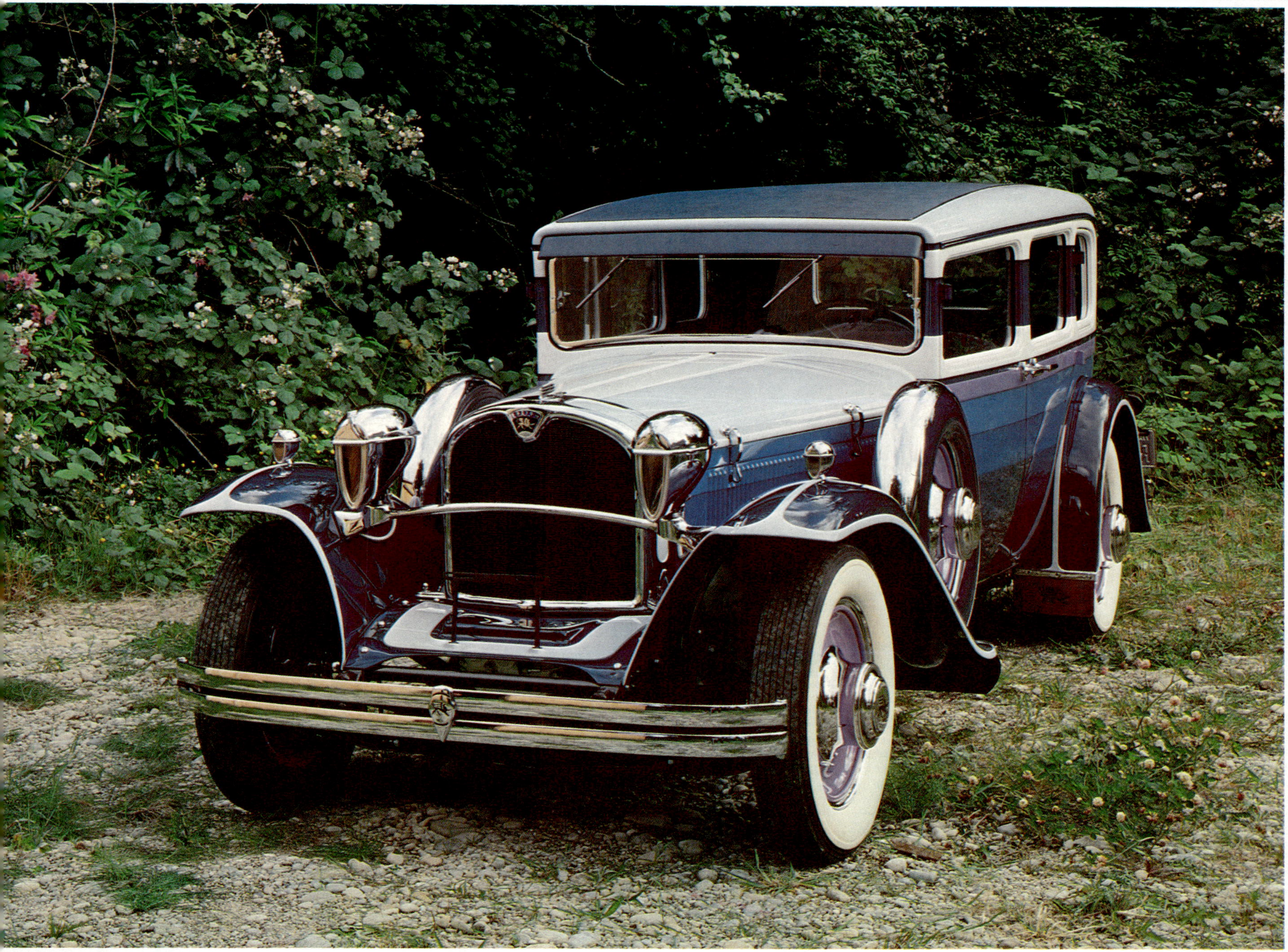

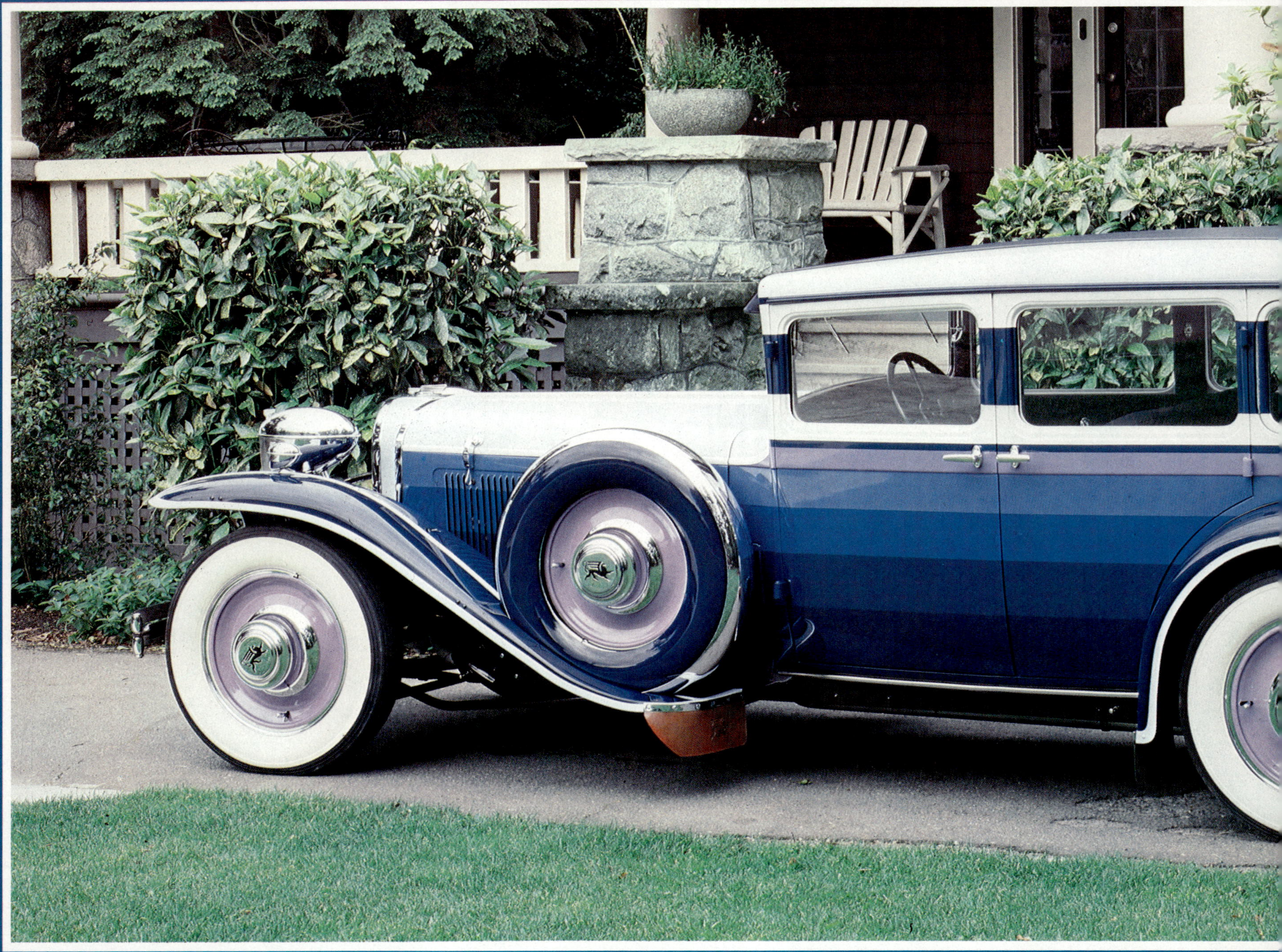

been sadly vitiated by use and abuse and hyperbole. All cars, we are told, are low, but the eye-arresting lowness of the Ruxton is not an optical illusion but a genuine lowness ingeniously attained by a ten-inch reduction in car and body height alike, yet without a single compromise with standard road clearance or headroom."

The officers of New Era Motors found another ingenious means of dramatizing the Ruxton's low height, the custom body colorings of New York stage designer and interior decorator Josef Urban. Urban's designs called for eight horizontal bands in graduated tones that shaded from light down to dark at the bottom of the body. Of course, the horizontality of this design, which was theoretically available in shades of blue, green, gray and maroon, made the unconventional lowness of the car even more apparent. Although the Urban design was intended to be available on all production sedans, this banding—which may remind some people of the layers of a pousse-café—actually appeared on only a few auto show specials.

Another of the Ruxton's strong selling points was its elaborate, carefully coordinated interior decoration. A glamorous advertisement in the November 1929 issue of Country Life features an illustration of the Ruxton sedan that had been embellished with Urban's distinctive banding. The effusive copy, which is laden with such words as "new," "today," "modern," and "contemporary," celebrates the upholstery and ornamental fittings specially designed for New Era Motors by F. Schumacher & Co.

According to the ad, the makers of Ruxton "have recognized that the highest type of machinery is not of sole importance in turning out a perfect automobile." Both sophisticated women and successful men regard their personal autos as extensions of themselves. "The really distinguished woman today," asserts the copy, "expects her car to provide a suitably smart background for her activities"; accordingly, it "should be decorated as tastefully—and modernly" as the public rooms of her house. Similarly, business executives now see to it that their automobile interiors embody "the same good taste and individuality that mark the new trend in office decoration."

To harmonize with Josef Urban's graduated ribbons of color, Schumacher especially recommended moiré "in rich harmonizing shades," although materials "reproduced from rare antique designs" and "the newest creations of prominent contemporary designers" were also available. In addition, corresponding decorative trimmings and automotive accessories could be ordered through Schumacher. These included toggles, road rails and gimps. If the overall effect was to be one of simplicity, that simplicity was nevertheless to have its own kind of elegance.

The 1930 sedan featured in this salon was intended for display car duty in the Los Angeles area, and bears serial number 1005, indicating that it was only the fifth Ruxton sedan to be built. Painstakingly restored by its owner, Doug Shinstine, over a period of four years, this car gives convincing proof to a West Coast dealer's assertion that, thanks to its revolutionary front wheel drive and avant-garde styling, the Ruxton represented "a sensational departure from conventional design."

PON
INCR

GH

C

BY KE

Color P
by Ro

**AC'S
DIBLE
OST
R**

**GROSS**

ography
Query

The sight is simply eerie. There's nothing like it on the road. The first view of Frank Kleptz' transparent Plexiglas 1940 Pontiac rolling down a highway is enough to make you pull off the road in disbelief. At a distance the plastic body is just a hazy gray outline. Moving closer, the x-ray-like appearance of this ghostly forty-year-old show car absolutely stops traffic. It's the twilight zone on wheels.

Not many Detroit experimental cars were built before the war, and still fewer have survived. Buick's Y-Job and Chrysler's Newports and Thunderbolts are notable exceptions. GM held on to its showcars, but some of the futuristic Chryslers eventually ended up in private hands. Display cars were a different matter. These cars weren't designed to be driven or sold. When their model year ended, their styling became obsolete overnight. Despite their expense and relatively short working lives, cut-away automotive exhibits detailing special features and unique construction have always been crowd pleasers.

Certainly Pontiac's pre-war World's Fair show cars carried the cut-away art to new dimensions. In keeping with the "World of Tomorrow" theme, GM's giant "Highways and Horizons" exhibit, one of the leading attractions of the 1939-40 New York World's Fair, was an optimistic attempt at predicting lifestyles twenty years ahead, surely a brave idea for a world on the brink of global war. Highlighting the GM pavillion, billed as "The Fair Within the Fair," was the "Futurama" exhibit. GM's product planners had pulled out all the stops to give the fairgoer a hint of new products to come. Many of the Futurama predictions have proven themselves remarkably accurate. But there was one glaring error. The company had guessed that there would be thirty-eight million vehicles on U.S. highways by 1960; the actual number turned out to be nearly double that prediction!

There was a lot to see that must have excited the visitors. In the "Previews of Progress" presentation, fairgoers marveled at "eyeglasses made of coal, air and water, cloth made of glass, the Frig-O-Therm that cooks an egg and freezes ice cream at the same time, the cordless radio microphone and the 'Talking Flashlight.'" All the GM divisions got into the act. Frigidaire's giant microscope dramatized the need for proper food preservation, Electromotive Corporation displayed a two thousand bhp diesel

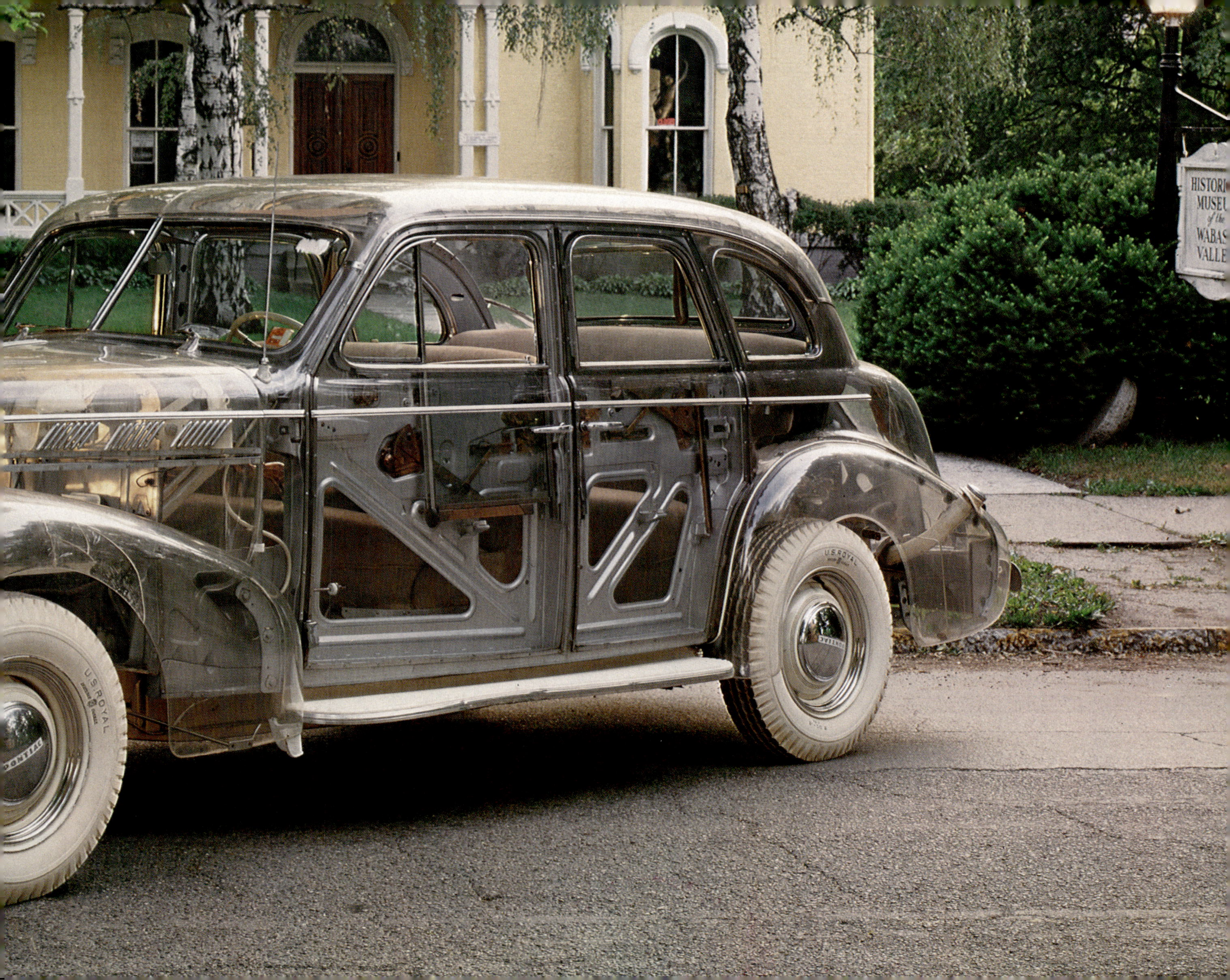
HISTORI
MUSEU
of the
WABAS
VALLE
U.S. ROYAL

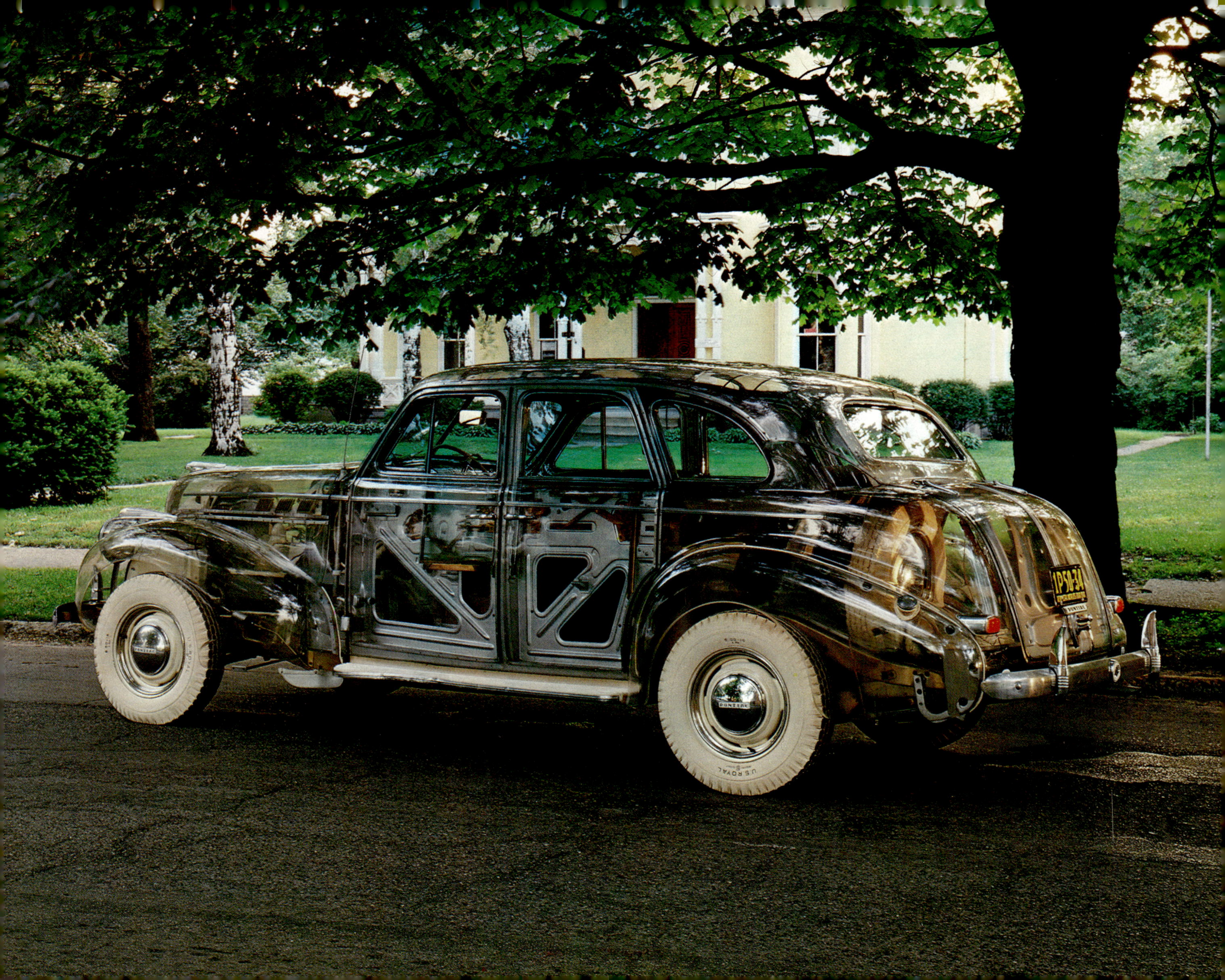
1P50-34

passenger locomotive with glass sides, and the entire GM automobile line was there to be admired.

And in the midst of everything was the incredible plastic Pontiac. Although no one remembers exactly, it's pretty certain that at least two of these transparent show cars were built, using Plexiglas for the first time in automobile construction. Curiously, the practical application of this material in regular production vehicles had not been considered by GM. These cars, along with Henry Ford's experimental soy bean oil plastic vehicles, were special one-off constructions. The use of Plexiglas had been inspired only by the material's transparency. Fisher Body had assembled the transparent cars to show off the structural components and running gear of their latest models. Fisher's Uni-Steel, Turret-top bodies were the big news across all the GM lines. The show cars' see-through construction also revealed the company's automatic door locks, concealed door hinges, independent front suspension, new sealed beam headlights, an improved safety hood lock, Duflex rear springs, Safti-Shift gearshift controls and a host of other new features.

Although the promotional names varied from division to division, many of these features were common to all GM cars. The Pontiac was chosen as an engineering showcase for the entire range. Copywriters had a lot of fun with the see-through show cars. As one publicity release put it, viewers would know "at a glance the hidden values that are built into Pontiac cars. See what you get when you buy a Pontiac." Pontiac got a lot of publicity mileage from its Plexiglas show cars. When they weren't touting features for the parent company, the transparent exhibits were trucked from coast to coast on exhibition tours. In between appearances at the 1939-40 New York Fair, one of the cars starred in the Golden Gate Exposition in San Francisco, and returned to the East Coast in January of 1940. The following month found a Plexiglas Pontiac in the deep South, on a tour of leading Pontiac dealerships, where its crowd-pulling capabilities made local newspaper headlines and encouraged on-site radio broadcasts.

There's still a lot of confusion about the Plexiglas Pontiacs. No one can verify who built the cars and just how many display vehicles were actually built. Some theorists originally held Dupont responsible for the body panels, since the chemical giant had experimented with similar plastics a year before the Pontiac appeared. Dupont's William C. Wall told Pontiac historian John A. Gunnell that his work in acrylic resins, or what became Lucite for the Delaware firm, did not include fabricating body panels for GM, and to his knowledge, Dupont had not been involved. The trail then led to Rohm & Haas in Philadelphia, the company responsible for the Plexiglas process and trademark. While Rohm & Haas company records could not confirm their involvement, Edmund Green, a former R & H public relations man now at Monsanto, recalled seeing photographs of the Pontiac show cars in his company's old files and remembered that GM had been supplied with Rohm & Haas plastic panels for later show cars. Green believes his company provided Fisher Body with the Plexiglas sections and the GM division did the rest. It's likely that Rohm & Haas supplied Plexiglas panels, but still unclear as to who molded them into replica Pontiac components.

The second part of the mystery is even more obscure. While John Gunnell and owner Frank Kleptz believe only one ghost car was built, there seems to be a lot of evidence to the contrary. Surviving photos from GM files and postcards from the San Francisco and New York Fairs show at least two body styles, with features from both the 1939 and 1940 models. *National Geographic* and *Popular Mechanics* both include photographs of the Plexiglas Pontiac in 1939, but the car is a 1939 B-bodied seven-window Deluxe sedan. San Francisco and New York World's Fair postcards and newspaper articles show the ghost car again, but now with 1940 Deluxe styling identical to our feature car.

The mystery gets more complicated at this point because GM files provided another series of photographs, this time of a 1940 five-window, C-bodied Special sedan. A close look at these photographs reveals structural details that differ from the Deluxe car. While the postcards appear to be heavily retouched, the B-bodied sedan has survived, so we know that car existed, and suspect that construction for the B-bodied version probably began in 1938, initially used 1939 panels and then was rebodied and detailed for 1940.

What of the five-window C-bodied car? It certainly looks as though there were at least two ghosts, perhaps three. And, if Rohm & Haas did supply their trademark product, Plexiglas, why did some contemporary magazine articles and show postcards refer to the car bodies as "glass-like plastic" or "transparent synthetic glass?"

In both the B and C-bodied cars, every part, including hoses, grommets, tires, mats and running boards, were molded in white rubber. The engine block, horns, air-cleaner, and numerous other mechanical components were painted white. This clever bit of detailing helped to popularize the name "ghost car." Structural components and running gear also merited special treatment befitting a GM display vehicle. Chrome, nickel, and copper plating abound. At what was obviously considerable expense, the instrument panel, window surrounds, and all the nuts and bolts were chromed. The cost of the car is estimated at $25,000 in 1939. The surviving ghost must have been a nice tax write-off. GM donated it to the Smithsonian Institution when the World's Fair ended. From that point, the car's history is well documented. The Plexiglas Pontiac was displayed in Washington until 1948. Then, when its styling became dated, it was sold to H & H Pontiac of Gettysburg, Pennsylvania. Fourteen years later, another Pennsylvania Pontiac dealer, Arnold Motors of Carlisle, acquired the car and installed full seats to replace the original cut-away cushions. In October of 1973, Donald Barlup of New Cumberland, Pennsylvania bought the car and promptly disassembled the panels for cleaning. At the time, the car only had seventy miles on the odometer and was missing the driveshaft, another mystery. Barlup sold the Pontiac to old car dealer Leo Gephart who in turn sold the show car to Frank Kleptz.

The ghost car is slated for additional restoration work. Over the years, some of the plastic panels have cracked and split. The Pontiac can be driven, but owner Kleptz reports that "it's murder on a hot day." Apparently the sun shines in and "bakes" the occupants. Road stones can easily damage and scratch the Plexiglas panels so it's unlikely the car will ever roll up much mileage. Besides, after the engine has run awhile, the plastic hood begins to sag ever so imperceptibly—but regains its shape after the car cools off.

Fisher Body's early Plexiglas experiments, at the dawn of the plastic age, could have been the first of a long series of plastic-bodied automobiles from Detroit. However, the idea was not deemed practical. Instead the pioneer efforts became another show curiosity—and a most intriguing mystery.✥

# W. F. BRADLEY

- JOURNALIST
- HISTORIAN
- CATALYST

## BY GRIFFITH BORGESON

*Your feeling that you might come and see me is most pleasing. You should understand, however, that I am in no position to entertain. When I left my little flat early in July, it was to go to the baker's—back in ten minutes. Instead, an ambulance took me to hospital with a double fracture of the pelvis. I was carrying out modifications to my living room and left a shambles behind me.*

*After a month in hospital I asked to be taken home. An ambulance brought me here and two huskies carried me upstairs. I can move about, providing I push a chair before me. I have no pain and I calculate that I ought to be able to walk unaided by the end of the month. Thus I have loads of time, even if it is all I do possess, and your company would be most welcome.*

This letter, signed W.F.B., was dated August 8th, 1965, meaning that its writer was heading into his ninetieth year. I had first made contact with him in 1959, while still living in my native California, and his correspondence had been a delight. Now, having settled not far from him in the south of France, I was eager to establish face-to-face contact with this personage, the dean of motoring journalists in the English language. It was toward the end of the month that I knocked on the door of his pleasant apartment overlooking the Mediterranean from the hills of Roquebrune, to the east of Monte Carlo.

His appearance had not changed greatly from that captured in various photos of him that I had seen in ancient magazines. He was small, lean, bird-like in build. There was nothing cocky about his air, but it projected great self-assurance and authority. Kindness and decency were easy to sense, along with strength of character and no inclination to turn away from a good fight. I believe that his accident was due to having been bowled over by a hurtling Vespa at nearby Menton. I was astonished by his recovery from such a very grave injury. A couple of charming, fortyish French ladies who dwelt in the same building were fond of him and fussed over and pampered him. But he was damned glad to have some masculine companionship. I got his Fiat *Millecento* running and we celebrated that evening by taking the ladies out to dinner, I performing the duties of chauffeur. It was his first outing since the accident and it was on that upbeat, festive note that our in-person relationship began.

That three-day visit was so fascinating and instructive that it was followed by others until, in failing health in 1969, this new old friend went to live with his son, better known as Jimmy, in the region of Toulouse. Early on I learned to regard this splendid veteran not merely as one of the most important automotive writers of all time, with a unique record of a half-century of continuous productivity, I also came to recognize in him an important actor in, and shaper of, automotive history. For these combined reasons I took a very strong interest in W.F.B.'s whole life story. Then, at the very end of his days, he wrote a long, family-oriented autobiography, which Jimmy kindly permitted me to read. Here, then, is my outline of one of the most remarkable careers in the entire field of automotive letters.

William Fletcher Bradley was born in Scarborough, Yorkshire on March 8th, 1876. The only fond memory of that part of what he called "the grim north" was the sea, which he adored and wanted to follow as a career. But his ailing father failed as a plumber, then as a baker, and there never was a penny to spare in the household. So much for the sea, since it took a certain investment to become an apprentice merchant seaman. He was not interested in becoming merely a deck hand and "there was too much soldiering in the Navy."

His mother managed to keep the family, including two daughters, on the brink of subsistence by taking in lodgers. W.F.B. had a small amount of elementary schooling but had to help with the survival of the group, beginning at a tender age. He worked approximately as a slave at a series of atrocious purgatories until his health began to deteriorate badly. Once, when he was perhaps twelve, he applied for a job, was looked over contemptuously and told, "We advertised for a boy, not a corpse."

This was righteous Protestant country, of course,

For Safe Night Driving
RUSHMORE
LENS MIRROR SEARCHLIGHTS
THE "LIFE BOAT"
Aerocar

*The 1907 Glidden Tour. Left and above: Bradley with Amos G. Batchelder, editor of* The Automobile *and a person once described by Bradley as one of the kindest men who ever lived. Below: a puncture stop near Canton, Ohio. Their air-cooled Aerocar did not survive the ordeal of the tour.*

and the family was Wesleyan. To show emotion, sentiment or affection was considered to be degenerate, and these manifestations of humanity were rigorously excluded from the family environment. What was ever-present was grinding, abject poverty. Many men, young and less young, sought escape in drink, where went such miserable earnings as fell their way. W.F.B., haunted and obsessed, determined to escape this fate by making something of himself. He had a fierce, innate pride, despised the injustice of the prevailing caste system, very close to the bottom of which he found himself condemned to live and die.

The family moved or fled to Leeds, "a grimy, smoky town on the banks of the River Aire, a river so polluted that in reality it was an open sewer." There, one of his mother's boarders worked as a reporter-typesetter on the local newspaper and from him this ragged child learned that it was possible to start in the print shop and to move from there into editorial work. In fact, many small-town newspapers were written, edited and printed by one and the same man. Being a journalist fitted W.F.B.'s aspirations and at age thirteen he apprenticed himself to a printer for seven years, with a starting pay of little or nothing. One of the things which impressed him most then was that no one, his parents in particular, took the slightest interest in what he did. All was left to chance.

He quickly learned that apprenticeship was not a form of training but, rather, a device which assured employers of dirt-cheap labor and the trade union of an elite status for its initiates. The boy did not let this discourage him. He took night classes in typesetting, shorthand, arithmetic, algebra and, because it attracted him for some fateful reason, French. He read, "considerably and studiously." By the time he was seventeen he had won the highest typesetter's rating that England offered, and was able to command five shillings a week. Soon this rose to all of eight and six, and he was self-supporting at last. He finished his apprenticeship on his twentieth birthday, whereupon his income jumped to a grandiose thirty-two and six a week. Rolling in wealth, he bought a bicycle and began getting stories printed in cycling periodicals. And he spent a month in London, which he found to be a cold and heartless city, where he completed a course in Linotype operation.

In November 1901 W.F.B. answered an ad for a

165

compositor placed by a small English-language press in Paris, and was hired at a good wage. The city fascinated him, and he loved it. His "health, which had always been precarious in England, became perfect in France." In April 1903 he married the love of his life, Maggie Nicol, a Scottish girl two years younger than he, whom he had met in Leeds. She responded to France at least as strongly as he did. He was still only a journeyman printer, but life had become a glorious adventure for them both.

Then it happened. An English friend named Vingoe, living in Paris, had the idea of sending news items, translated from French sources, to automotive magazines in the United States. He found the address of *Motor Age*, in Chicago, and that of *The Automobile*, in New York. Since the two publications were in direct competition with each other Vingoe had to make a choice and for some reason it was *Motor Age*. He suggested that Bradley give *The Automobile* a try. He did, it clicked, and thus began his fifty or so consecutive years with the Class Journal Company. Let it be noted parenthetically that *The Automobile* changed its name to *Automotive Industries* in 1917 and that *Motor Age* was absorbed by the latter during the following year.

To get a better idea of what he was writing about W.F.B. took lessons on a Darracq car and obtained a driver's license. The start of his professional career can be regarded as the start of the Paris-Madrid road race in May 1903. He records how it was in the opening chapter of his book, *Motor Racing Memories*. When he speaks there of "Minette" he is using his pet name for Maggie. It means kitten and darling in French.

"The great material move in our life in France came when the *Daily Mail* decided, in 1904, to issue a Continental edition. I was taken on as an assistant proofreader. This situation was a wonderful step upwards, for not only did my wages increase from 60 to 80 francs a week, but I did not begin work until between eight and nine in the evening, and I was free at three in the morning. Another advantage was that I was gaining experience in journalism and approaching the time when I should become a fully fledged journalist. Rising at noon, I was free for the whole of the afternoon, thus having time to attend to work for *The Automobile*. And at about that time I had the

*Bradley's first car, a 1909 Sizaire & Naudin. Maggie holds Jimmy; Margaret ("Daisy") sits on floorboards. Above: with Harry Farman, in on the ground floor of aviation. Below: a photograph often said to show W.F. Bradley together with Jules Goux. The former is really legendary journalism czar Charles Faroux.*

good fortune to come into contact with George Sharp, who asked me to become Paris correspondent of *The Motor*. I had all the work I could handle and was doubtless earning more as a writer than as a proofreader. This struggle against poverty which had so obsessed me had ceased to exist. Enthusiasm for my work had taken the place of fear."

W.F.B.'s first really big assignment occurred at this period: covering both the elimination trials and the race for the cup offered in 1905 by James Gordon Bennett, publisher of the New York *Herald*, along with its Paris edition. Next came a move from the *Daily Mail* to the *Herald*, working as makeup man, and for a sumptuous 90 francs a week. W.F.B. found a new sort of world among these Americans. "There was a spirit of equality entirely absent on the *Daily Mail*. Socially no man stood higher than any other." Then, in the fall of 1906, *The Automobile's* editor, Amos G. Batchelder, came to France to cover the Grand Prix. The two men became excellent friends and "Batch" offered W.F.B. the job of assistant editor if he would come to New York. Leaving France was an agonizing decision to have to make, but in early January 1907 W.F.B. presented himself in the magazine's office in the Flat Iron Building, on 21st and Broadway in New York City. He found the atmosphere there to be "even more friendly and democratic than at the *Herald*."

During the fourteen months that he remained there W.F.B. became a thoroughly professional journalist and, in addition, acquired an intimate knowledge of American conditions and of the motorization movement in the U.S.A. "Batch" liked to use him for competition coverage, and W.F.B. became acquainted personally with most of the important drivers, car owners, organizers, and officials active in motor racing in the eastern United States. He continued to write for *The Motor* and became American correspondent for *L'Auto* of Paris. He was very content where he was, but another baby was expected and Maggie wanted to return to Paris, and that was decisive. W.F.B. continued to write for *The Automobile* there, saying later that "during the 50 years I worked for the firm I never felt any necessity for a written agreement and there never was a shadow of a dispute." While in the States he participated in the 1907 Glidden Tour, which made him a convert to

167

*World War I: Bradley with Eddie Rickenbacker and an unidentified friend; (below): Avenue Montaigne, Paris, 1918. Bradley brought many of these Fiats from Turin for the use of American Aviation HQ in France. Right: in the early Twenties, at the summit of his field, Bradley chats with Felice Nazzaro.*

the American better roads movement. He witnessed the start of the New York-to-Paris race in Times Square in February and covered its finish in Paris at the end of July.

On his return to France W.F.B. bought his first car, a Sizaire & Naudin one-lunger the price of which was $590, without top. The auto editor of the Paris *Herald* died, and W.F.B. was selected to replace him. This position carried great prestige in the eyes of the European industry and it also brought him into contact with prominent American manufacturers, engineers and motorists who came to Paris, then the world's motor capital. The age of practical heavier-than-air aviation set in and W.F.B. added that aspect of motorization to his stock-in-trade. He came to know all of the great early pioneers, including the Wrights, Bleriot, the Farman brothers, Voisin and Curtiss, and he covered most of the epic-making early flights and meetings. In the automotive field he knew everyone, as far away as the boondocks of Strasbourg, then in Germany. He did the first reportage on the first production Bugatti for *The Motor* in 1910, as he would report on the last one in *The Autocar* in 1952. When he was fired by eccentric James Gordon Bennett in 1910, the *Herald* job no longer mattered. He was an internationally respected personage, with markets waiting avidly for everything he might choose to write.

He knew the drivers and pilots, the engineers and the manufacturers, the total milieu. He was on excellent terms with Louis Coatalen, Louis Delage, Marc Birkigt, and hosts of all-but-anonymous designers who nevertheless played vital roles in the evolution of the automobile. For a good while speedboats were the most important test benches for automotive and aero engines and he followed the all-important speed weeks at Monaco year after year. He knew the drivers of the Peugeot team and was not far from the action when *Les Charlatans* (AUTOMOBILE *Quarterly*, Volume XI, Number 3) launched an engineering revolution with the world's first hemi-head twin-cam engine.

Known as he was and respected by all the right people in the States ("Batch" had become a power in the AAA), in 1910 or '11 W.F.B. was appointed European Delegate of the American Automobile Association. He was the first representative of the AAA Contest Board to sit on the International Sporting Commission of the AIACR, renamed the

FIA after World War II. He held that highly important post continuously until 1937.

In 1912 Carl Fisher, the tycoon among whose creations was the Indianapolis Motor Speedway, realized correctly that top-flight foreign competition was exactly what was needed to swell the box-office receipts of his two-year-old five-hundred-mile race. Fisher asked the A.A.A.'s C.A. Sedwick, then on his way to Europe, to contact W.F.B. to see what he could do. With the American in tow, Bradley braced Georges Boillot, the organizational intellect behind the entire Charlatan operation, and sold him on sending two cars to Indianapolis. It was not easy, due to the fly-by-night reputation of many American race promoters, but W.F.B. pulled it off and it had exactly the result which Fisher had foreseen. From that time onward, Bradley had yet another iron always in the fire. Fisher appointed him not the Speedway's but his own personal representative in Europe. This relationship lasted as long as European entries remained competitive at Indianapolis.

Never neglecting his journalistic activites, W.F.B. went on cultivating new ones. After Jules Goux' Peugeot win at Indy in 1913, Boillot decided personally to head an official team the following year. Fisher wanted still more good foreign entries and so Bradley organized an équipe of his own: a pair of borrowed 1913 Delages for René Thomas and Albert Guyot, a borrowed Peugeot for Arthur Duray, and an Excelsior for Josef Christiaens. He travelled with and managed that team and it finished first, second, third and ninth—a fantastic performance which ripped off the lion's share of the world's richest purse.

Ten weeks later war broke out. Bradley was thirty-eight years old and full of fight. He volunteered his car and his own services as a driver and was enrolled at various times in the British, Belgian and Italian armies. Carrying out all manner of missions he also was able to observe and write about the urgent new subject of the military utilization of motor vehicles. Eventually he wound up as an ambulance driver in Italy where, as a Second Lieutenant in the Italian army, he saw considerable front-line action near Gorizia. As a volunteer he was able to move from one hot spot to another, observing and reporting back to his editors. Then Fiat contacted him, on the strength of his 1914 exploit, and engaged him to manage a team

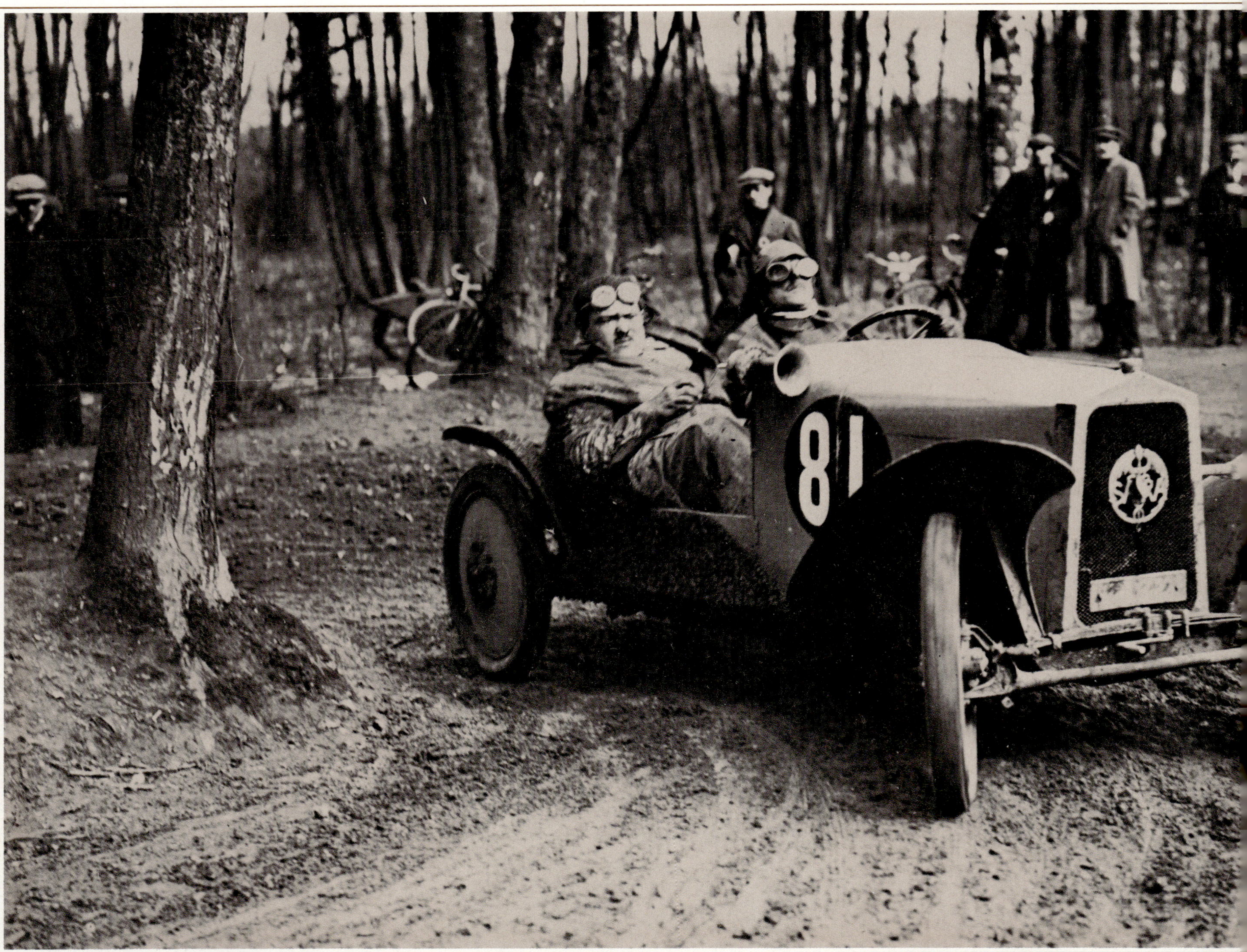
81

*Bradley at the wheel of the SARA car in a race at St. Cucufa in 1921 or '22, moments before an accident from which he barely recovered. Above: Bradley drove this Talbot with four-wheel brakes in one of the Paris-Nice rallies in the early Twenties. 1923: observer Bradley rides in a Delage in a Paris-Madrid demonstration run.*

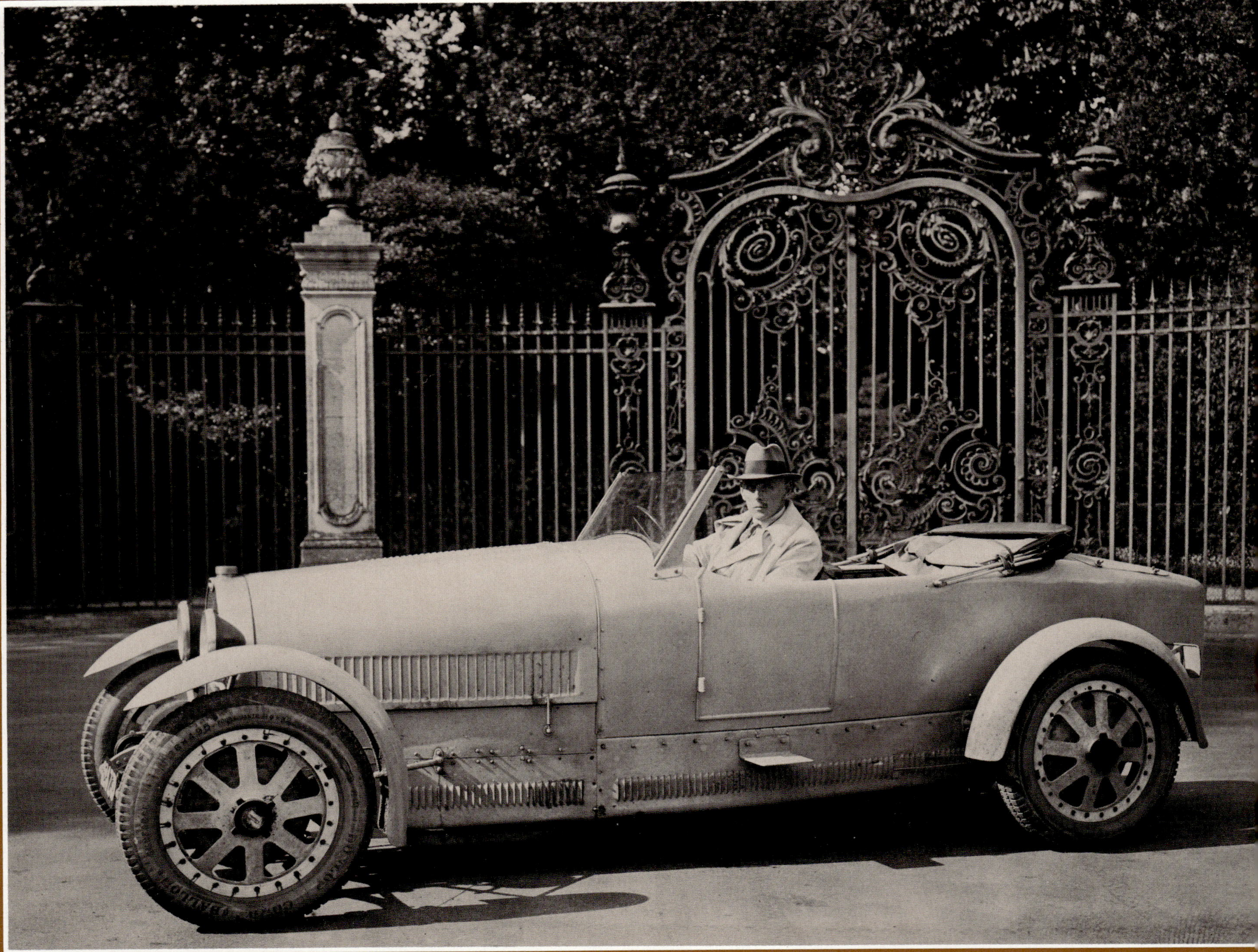

of cars for the 1917 Indianapolis 500. The machines were in Genoa, awaiting shipment, when the United States entered the war and the big race was suspended for the duration.

For two years W.F.B. had been reporting to Howard Coffin, of the Hudson Motor Car Company and then in charge of the National Defense Committee in Washington. His reports dealt with the use of motor vehicles under conditions of war, and modifications to them which field experience indicated should be made. Bradley returned to Paris and was there to meet Major R.C. Bolling, head of the U.S. Aeronautical Commission, when it arrived in June. The Commission was charged with forming and equipping aircraft squadrons manned by American personnel and to engage them in the combat effort. This included the acquisition of advanced designs for airframes and aero engines to be built in the U.S.A., as well as the formation of supporting car, truck and motorcycle pools. W.F.B. was, of course, a heaven-sent expert on all those matters and he was taken immediately into the Commission with the rank and pay of a Captain, but with civilian status. This arrangement had the virtue of permitting him to counsel and correct persons of higher rank.

One of his first acts was to bring the Commission—he always called it the Bolling Mission—together with Ettore Bugatti, who then was working in Paris on the development of his famous sixteen-cylinder *moteur-canon*. "But I had nothing to do with the acceptance of those engines," he told me, also referring to the earlier straight-eight which was included in the famous deal. "That was the responsibility of the Commission's dollar-a-year men, such as Marmon and Gorrell."

The first member of the American Expeditionary Force to be killed in that war is said to have been the soldier who got in the way of the original U16's propeller while it was undergoing tests. The engine turned out to be a failure which cost the American taxpayer in the neighborhood of $5 million. It did serve to give Bugatti worldwide fame and to bankroll his new start following the war.

Never will we know the extent of W.F.B.'s catalytic influence upon important international affairs at this epoch, but it must have been considerable. For example, in his Smithsonian Annals of Flight book, *The Liberty Engine, 1918-1942*, Lt. Col. P.S. Dickey III tells how, on the

*Bradley in his Bugatti T.43 Grand Sport about 1928. Above: W.F.B. with Nuvolari, probably in 1936 when he won the Vanderbilt Cup race for Alfa Romeo. Group picture taken at LeMans in 1951; artist Peter Helck is on Bradley's immediate right. Helck's son Jerry stands on other side of his father.*

A LUNCHEON

TO MARK THE CONCLUSION OF

MR. W. F. BRADLEY'S SURVEY OF THE LONDON-ISTANBUL ROUTE

CHAIRMAN: SIR JOHN D. SIDDELEY, C.B.E., J.P.　　MAY FAIR HOTEL, 21ST JULY, 1933

*May Fair Hotel menu: In 1933 Bradley, accompanied by his daughter, made a survey of routes between London and Istanbul on behalf of the Automobile Association. He drove a 5-liter Siddeley Special.*

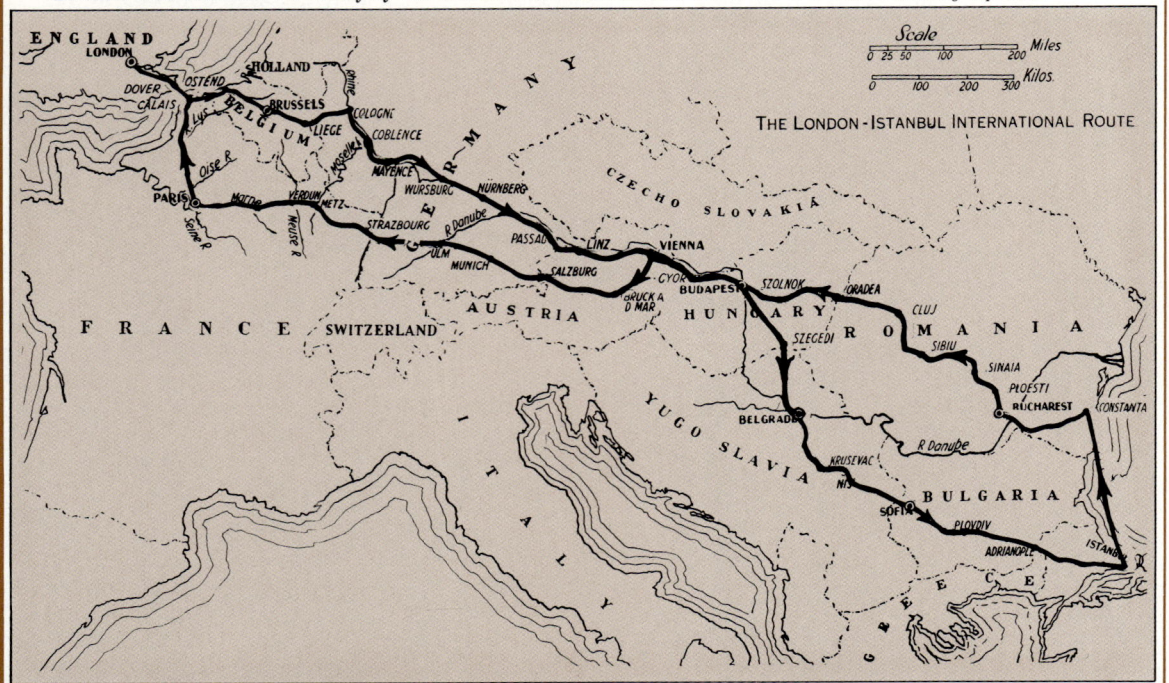

THE LONDON-ISTANBUL INTERNATIONAL ROUTE

---

morning of May 27th, 1917, Jesse G. Vincent, Packard's chief engineer, read an article by W.F.B. in the latest issue of *The Automobile*. It described the chaos caused for French military aviation by its dependence upon thirty-four different types of engine. Vincent had the vision of a single, standardized aero engine for the American Air Force. It was Sunday, and he went to see Packard's president, Alvan Macauley, at his home, and was in Washington the following morning, presenting to Howard Coffin, now head of the Aircraft Production Board, the basic concept of America's famous Liberty engine program. The incident was reported by *Automotive Industries* for November 1st, 1917 under the headline: "W.F. Bradley In Air Service—Now Technical Expert for American Aviation in France." He retained this capacity until the end of the war. His duties took him frequently to Turin and Milan, to Fiat and Isotta Fraschini. Italy was an ardent country, like France, for which he had a very strong attachment.

With the war's end Fiat engaged W.F.B. to establish and operate an English-language Fiat press service, based in Paris. This provided him with offices at a swank address in the Champs Elysées and took him to Turin at least once a month. He of course came to know the great Giovanni Agnelli and such illustrious Fiat engineers as Guido Fornaca and Carlo Cavalli. He continued to conduct this PR operation until it was dropped by Fiat in 1933, probably as a consequence of nationalistic government policy at the time. W.F.B. managed not to let it interfere with his myriad other activities.

The fact that the best coverage, by far, of the revolutionary Ballot straight-eights for Indianapolis in 1919 (AUTOMOBILE *Quarterly*, Volume XV, Number 2) was signed by W.F.B. is proof that he had an inside track on that historic operation. An elaborate legend was created around the situation, with the probable main purpose of smoke-screening the fact that a racing program had been in the works while men still were dying on the battlefields. Bradley's protégé, Indy-winning René Thomas, was the ostensible ring-leader of the operation and ex-*Charlatan* engineer Ernest Henry of course was responsible for design. It is my long and carefully considered belief that this program, based upon the finest racing cars the world had seen up to that point, was masterminded by Bradley, who sold it to

Ballot. Unfortunately, he had gravely overestimated Thomas' executive and organizational competence, and thus a perfect plan for again walking off with the bulk of Indianapolis' fat purse was thwarted. Ernest Ballot's mistake was in accepting W.F.B.'s confidence in Thomas, and his fury must have been shattering. He would have told W.F.B. to get out of sight, probably adding that any contractual arrangement which may have existed between them had been voided by W.F.B.'s own bad judgment. Something along these lines is needed to explain the vendetta which the journalist carried out against Ballot for the rest of his days.

In 1920 W.F.B. had another fling at Indianapolis, this time with a pair of Grégoire cars, driven by Jean Porporato and Jack Scales. Again he placed his bets badly. As he used to say, "I had the best team of all time in 1914 and the worst of all time in 1920." Scales was unable to qualify and Porporato was ordered off the track because he and his car were obstructing traffic.

Very soon after the Armistice W.F.B. accepted an offer to write for *The Autocar* and the Iliffe group of publications, and for the double of the rates which he had been paid by *The Motor* and Temple Press. It was not so much the money that induced him to make the change as it was the consummate indifference with which the best of his wartime work, and that achieved at the greatest risk, had been received. He remained loyal to *The Autocar* for the rest of his life.

Bradley had the distinction of saving the first postwar GP of the Automobile Club de France, which he did in his typical wry style. In 1921, just a couple of days before the closing of entries, he received, in his capacity as the AAA Contest Board's man in Paris, a cablegram from Fred Duesenberg requesting him to enter three of his cars in the race. Apparently Duesenberg was unaware of the entry fee of $1000 per car, for there was no mention of it. What was worse, post-entries were required to pay a one hundred percent penalty. Bradley caught the ACF's René de Knyff on the sidewalk in front of the club's palatial offices in the Hotel Crillon, Place de la Concorde. Trying to spare Duesenberg the penalty he said, "I've got three good American cars for your race, if you'll give me a couple of days to get the money together. I happen to know that the Fiats which are entered will not take the start. That Talbot-Darracq will make it is

*Bradley in Istanbul on a 1938 tour in a Grégoire-designed, Hotchkiss-built Amilcar Compound, and in Durban, South Africa with a Millecento presented by Fiat when he retired from full-time journalism.*

*Bradley receiving the Harold Pemberton Trophy of the Guild of Motoring Writers in 1960.*

very uncertain. That will leave you with three Ballots and a meaningless Mathis, and you can't run a race under those conditions."

The Chevalier de Knyff stared at him in offended silence for a long moment, then rolled his eyes up at the historic building and said, "You might just as well ask me to set fire to this place."

The money did arrive soon enough, and long before the final closing date for post-entries. But Bradley left it in the bank and would give de Knyff no news. Then, on the last day and just as the ACF offices were closing, W.F.B. walked in, coolly laid the entry forms and a check for $8000 in front of de Knyff and announced, "Duesenberg is entering four cars. Congratulations."

Bradley's close relationship with Louis Delage goes back at least to 1908 and the Delage/Guyot victory in the GP des Voiturettes de l'ACF at Dieppe. In 1919 Delage took the controversial step of adopting four-wheel brakes as standard equipment on all his cars and was determined to demonstrate their efficacy and safety himself. He did this by attempting to make the almost 1000 km run from Paris to Nice in a single day, something which seemed insane at the time because much of the road was in deplorable condition after years of wartime neglect. He invited W.F.B. to come along as an observer, and Bradley kept a log of the trip, certifying to its accuracy. They did it, leaving Paris at dawn and having dinner in Nice.

It was perhaps in 1923 that Louis Delage decided to repeat his demonstration of four-wheel brakes, but on the scale of a Tour de France, and again W.F.B. went along as observer. They started from Paris, went up to Cherbourg, down the Brittany coast, across to Nice, then up the eastern frontier into Alsace and the north of France, then back to Paris. They did it in five days, occasionally getting a thousand kilometers into the day. "Everything went well," W.F.B. remembered, "until the last day, when we were about ten miles outside of Paris and stopped to piddle by the side of the road. I walked around the car and noticed that one of the Rudge hubs had split. It would have broken right off within a mile or two, right on the main road leading into Paris, in heavy traffic, and everyone would have seen a Delage there, lying on its side. We changed it, saved by sheer luck."

It was in 1921 or '22 that W.F.B. drove a SARA two-seater in a hairy "endurance and reliability trial" in the Bois de St. Cucufa. The car's tubular front axle fell apart in full flight and the machine crashed violently against a tree. Bradley came very close to death on this occasion and went racing no more. "They immediately changed the axle," he said. "Thus, at my expense, racing had improved the breed."

I am not certain of when W.F.B. began covering the Targa Florio but it well may have been in 1906, when the first of them all took place. Vincenzo Florio, an international playboy of a very constructive sort, knew Paris as well as he knew his native Palermo, and he and his wife and W.F.B. and Maggie became lifelong friends. Prior to one of the early races young Florio suggested to Bradley that the best way to cover a race is to take part in it. Bradley agreed, and the tradition began of Florio always turning over his personal car, Number 00, and his driver, Mario, to his friend for the race. It was a privilege that was reserved for him alone, he recalled, and it had a great deal to do with his excellent coverage of that formidable contest.

"It gave me an insight into the race," he told me, "that no one else ever had. The drivers never objected to it. Of course we took very great care never to be in their way. We never went into a turn if there was a car likely to overtake us. And we used to pick up the drivers whose cars had been wrecked. The two of us would go out and often come back with six. And we'd get their stories of the race. We really lived the race as nobody else did."

In his great book, *The Grand Prix Car* (1949), one

of Lawrence Pomeroy's key references was a technical paper by E.W. Sisman which was published in *The Automobile Engineer* for July 1927. On this authority Pom was able to trace the origins of the modern straight-eight engine back to Bugatti, saying that Ernest Henry had worked on Bugatti's aero eight and U16 in Paris during the war. I never was able to confirm this employment stint of Henry's but after the appearance of "The Charlatan Mystery" in AUTOMOBILE *Quarterly* I received a friendly and informative letter from engineer Sisman, who had taken his retirement in Australia. I asked him what had been his source for these specific data and he told me that it was an article in *The Autocar* for May 7th, 1921 by—of course—W.F. Bradley.

The article is titled "Experts and Straight-Eight Engines—Tracing the Origins of the Present Favour of the Eight-cylinder in-line Engine for Racing." Also in headline type are the words "M. Bugatti the Initiator." In my recent book on Bugatti I suggest that this piece of important editorial publicity probably was related to the impending introduction of Bugatti's first eight-cylinder road and racing models, and suggest that:

"In this belated effort to transfer the leadership of Ballot and Duesenberg to Bugatti, W.F.B. included alleged interviews with two experts: Henry and Ettore. It is quite possible that, after seeing this article in print, Henry, a quiet but violent man, gave Bradley the thrashing of his life. This at last would explain why W.F.B. at this period ceased his references to Henry as a great and brilliant engineer and began treating him as 'a mere draftsman'."

The only European entries at Indianapolis in 1922—aside from a prewar Peugeot—were two Ballots, taken over by Jules Goux. The following year, however, W.F.B. had his work cut out for him, with what he called "getting together" the Bugatti team for Indianapolis. It consisted of Martin de Alzaga, Prine de Cystria, Pierre de Vizcaya, Raoul Riganti, and Count Louis Zborowski. For track racing the cars were hopelessly outclassed by the two-liter Millers, only de Cystria going the whole distance and finishing in ninth place.

The rapid specialization of track racing in the U.S.A. made it increasingly impossible for Americans and Europeans to participate in each other's speed contests. When W.F.B. took Pietro Bordino and a GP Fiat to the States in 1925, it was all finished. Both the car and the driver were splendid, but neither stood the faintest chance of making a good showing against the Americans on *their* ground. The Europeans stopped crossing the Atlantic for nothing and Bradley's last chore for the AAA and the Speedway during the Twenties was setting up Louis Chiron's participation in the 1929 500, at the wheel of the world's road-racing champion car, the divine 1.5 liter Delage. His seventh place was a humiliating disappointment and Bradley's Indianapolis responsibilities simply withered away.

However, Speedway manager Pop Myers sent him a present with which to finish off the 1929 season in the form of Leon Duray and his Packard

*Bradley at Roquebrune during a visit by Ronald Barker and his Lancia Dilambda in 1965.*

Cable Special Millers. W.F.B. said that he had "managed both Durays—Arthur and Leon." Leon's program when he came to Paris that summer was keyed to the European debut of the L29 Cord car, a specimen of which was included in Leon's baggage. The front-wheel-drive racing cars would be used by Leon to generate publicity for the sensational new commercial product.

When I acquired the Packard Cable Specials from Bugatti in 1959 I entered into correspondence with W.F.B., seeking details of their past. Later we spoke of them on many occasions, but the Cord element of the story never was alluded to by him. It would appear that Duray had used Bradley merely in connection with his quite successful record attempts at Linas-Montlhéry, near Paris, and other favors, such as coping with the formalities of entry in the Monza Grand Prix that September, which happened to be run by Vincenzo Florio.

What went wrong between Duray and Bradley I never could learn. Each felt brutally misused by the other. In 1951 Duray wrote to me saying that he wanted to tell me the story, which he said actually was quite funny, but death took him before that could be accomplished. Bradley said that Duray had taken to the bottle very seriously and that his behavior in Europe was atrocious. This was confirmed to me recently by Albert Guyot's son, André, who had replaced W.F.B. as Duray's guide and who accompanied him over the Alps to Monza, Duray wheeling the Cord in an unforgettable manner. André was not a witness to the transaction in which the Millers passed to Bugatti. Duray once told me, in passing, that his main reason for entering the Vanderbilt Cup Races at Roosevelt Raceway was that he expected Bradley to be there and hoped to have an opportunity to "accidentally" run him over. W.F.B. got his revenge by missing no opportunity during the rest of his career to do in Duray's character. Bradley's version of what had happened never was entirely coherent, partly due to the fact that old Arthur Duray had appeared out of the dim past at Monza in 1927, and he was confused with the then-celebrity Leon even in the track's own records.

The Twenties coincided with the material high point of W.F.B.'s career, culminating in the acquisition, in 1930, of the dream home that he and Minette had dreamed of having some day. It was located at 7, rue du Peintre Jérome in Bougival, a small community in rolling, wooded country a few miles west of Paris' Bois de Boulogne. With the closing of the Fiat PR operation in 1933 W.F.B. no longer had a downtown office. I gather that he worked from his beautiful home, and at a more serene pace.

It was in about 1933 that he made a notable trek from London to Istanbul and back in an Armstrong Siddeley. His daughter Margaret, more fondly known as Daisy, accompanied him to make sketches of the trip. She was an accomplished artist in pen and ink, water colors and oil painting. At this period W.F.B. began to cover the Alpine Trial each year. After the Targa Florio it seems to have been his favorite event; he became an active participant in it, doing quite well.

*The author's photograph of W.F.B. taken in the autumn of 1965, when he first visited him at Roquebrune.*

When George Eyston went to the Bonneville Salt Flats for the first time in 1935 he obtained Bradley's services as "manager" of the expedition. This provided W.F.B. with the material for his first book, *Speed on Salt*, published the following spring. Eyston contributed two of its chapters and the book was given a joint by-line. And at this period W.F.B. began to have or to seize the leisure to enjoy his lifelong passion for the sea, becoming an active yachtsman.

In the mid-Thirties old-time American racing driver George Robertson conceived the idea of reviving the Vanderbilt Cup road race and interested a group of New York investors in backing the plan. Engineer Art Pillsbury, designer of the best American board tracks and a pillar of the AAA Contest Board, was given the job of creating an enclosed road course for the purpose. Pillsbury went to Paris and contacted W.F.B., who obtained a Talbot from Tony Lago, with which the American visited every important European circuit. The result was the zero-karma Roosevelt Raceway on Long Island, which Pillsbury himself told me he considered to be the greatest failure of his career. Bradley, still the European delegate of the Contest Board, was given carte blanche for providing the European entries in both installments of the latter-day Vanderbilt, in 1936 and '37. He did the job with his usual well-seasoned professional competence but almost everything else went wrong, both years, and thus ended his quarter-century reign as one-man liaison between European and American motor racing.

In early 1938, aged 62, W.F.B. undertook the driving of a Hotchkiss-built Amilcar Compound from Paris to Algiers, Cairo, Jerusalem, Baghdad, Istanbul, Vienna, Strasbourg, London, and back to Paris; it took him about a month. And then came World War II.

It was in May 1940, after receiving early warning from Jimmy, somewhere in France with the RAF, that they decided to abandon their beloved Bougival, but too late. After a brief sejour near St. Malo they realized that no boats were going to waft them safely to the U.K. After considerable reflection W.F.B. and Maggie decided to sit tight and ride out the crisis in the home and country that were so dear to them. It was a disastrous choice of possible alternatives, for W.F.B. was picked up very soon by the occupying Germans and imprisoned as an enemy alien, under soul-wracking conditions. He supported this well enough until his Minette, too, was carried off to a mountain prison camp in the dead of winter. He deteriorated emotionally and physically until, after many months, Maggie was released and again could pay him rare visits. It was not until the end of 1943, when he was 68, that his captors gave him back his freedom. This was followed by a life of near-starvation until the Liberation in the summer of 1944.

One of W.F.B.'s first acts then was to offer his services and the use of his car to the British Embassy in Paris. He was placed in charge of its motor pool. "After our war experience in France," he wrote, "life in well-ordered England appeared to be a paradise." He and Maggie moved to a peaceful corner of the English countryside, only to find that "fifty years' absence had made us foreigners." Then they moved to Bournemouth. "But in this town class distinctions reigned complete. In a given street every house was like every other one, and the streets and avenues were marked out distinctly for people of certain income groups. It was all regimented."

W.F.B. resumed his writing career in England and, in 1947, had the excellent idea of persuading his very old friend, Ettore Bugatti, to collaborate with him in the preparation of a very thorough story of *Le Patron's* career. The date was set for the beginning of the series of daily interviews on which this biography was to be based. W.F.B. presented himself for the rendezvous in Paris, but Ettore was stricken at that moment with an illness from which he did not recover, dying on August 21st. Bradley knew much of the story from almost four decades of personal experience, and there were other well-placed sources who were eager to contribute to the effort. He received important help from Ernest Friderich, Dr. Espanet, L'Ebé and Roland Bugatti, and Ettore's personal secretary, Georges Clavel. He thus was able to complete, for publication in March 1948, the first important work in this important field. The fact that the book served as a medium for much mythology detracts in no way from its value and significance . . . if one is properly on guard.

W.F.B. and Maggie managed to stick it out in England until early 1950, then moved back to Vaucresson, a stone's throw from their well-loved Bougival. Aged 74, he continued to be active in automotive journalism and to cover his old Paris beat, with style and grace, until his wife's death on December 9th, 1953. Devastated, he no longer had incentive to work, formally broke his long-standing professional connections, and retired, to live with his son in Durban, South Africa. He found the Union "very interesting, alive and vital, in the manner of the United States." Of course he could not stay away from his old craft and he continued to produce the occasional article for publication in England and the U.S.A. It was in Durban that he wrote his third book, *Targa Florio—An authentic history of the famous motor race.*

But no place could take the place of France in W.F.B.'s old heart and in 1958, aged 82, he returned, purchasing the apartment at Roquebrune, where I had the privilege of basking in his astonishing knowledge. It was there that he completed his last book, *Motor Racing Memories, 1903-1921*, a marvelous collection of beautifully told tales of history lived at first hand. Its scope ranges from the Paris-Madrid to the Duesenberg victory at Le Mans. The book merited a much better reception than it in fact received.

As a man, my friend Bradley possessed the most absolute rectitude of character. He was a noble soul, spewed into an unspeakable environment, from which he extricated himself with great courage and honor. He was a sensitive, warm-hearted interpreter of the world around him. He was a journalist of the grand school of which France's Charles Faroux was the universally acknowledged dean. Bradley was its dean for the Anglo-Saxon world. When he turned his hand to the writing of history the journalistic spirit prevailed, as in the case of Faroux in *his* late years. Nevertheless, Bradley stands as one of the greatest chroniclers in what some unknown Frenchman has termed "this promethean literature of the automobile." In addition to that, there was his catalytic influence upon events, on which we have so little data. For example, twenty-four-hour racing was at its height when he was in the United States in 1907, and he covered more than one such event. He probably covered them for Faroux's *L'Auto*, among other publications, and may even have sold Faroux on the idea, which Faroux would apply later at Le Mans. I had this into-everything aspect of W.F.B.'s character in mind when, in the dedication of *The Classic Twin-Cam Engine*, I said that his role in automotive history was more important than we shall ever know. ✥

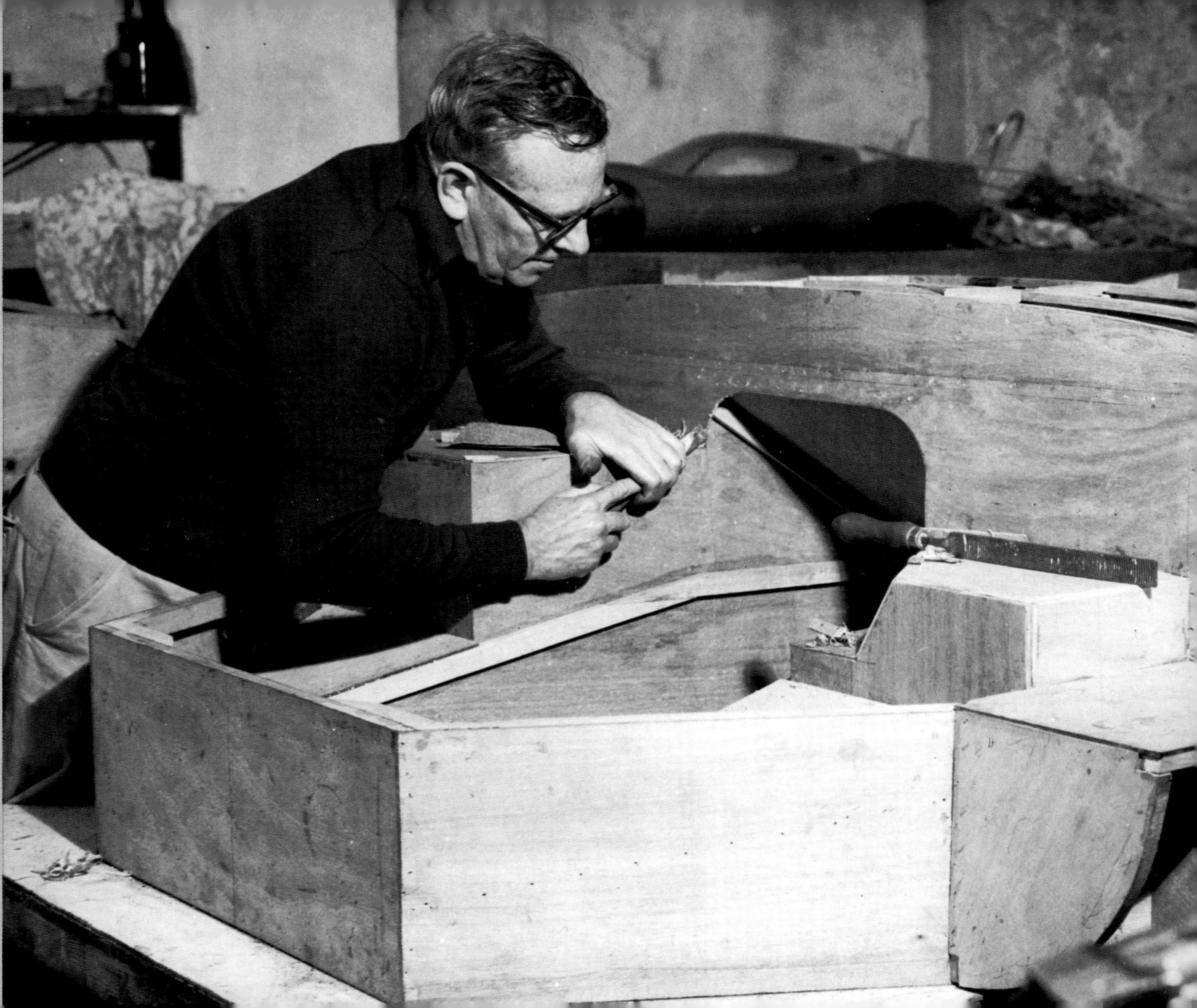

# THE WOODEN CHASSIS AUTOMOBILES OF FRANK COSTIN

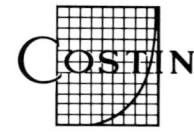

COSTIN

By Dennis Ortenburger
Color Photography by Neill Bruce

## THE EARLY YEARS

From 1955 until 1975 the title of automobile aerodynamicist was personified by one man: Frank Costin. His ability to make racing cars slice through the air better than their competitors became almost legendary, and his list of designs includes some of the most successful racers of modern times. The Lotus Marks 8, 9, 11 and Elite owed their streamlined shapes to his hand, as did the World Champion Formula I Vanwall and the Land Speed Record-breaking Speedwell Sprite. Unlike many of his predecessors, Costin endowed his shapes with an attribute essential to their success: aerodynamically induced high-speed stability. Unaided by tacked-on aerodynamic devices, his automobiles were known for both their remarkably high top speeds compared to cars with similar engine displacements, and their indifference to cross winds or ground effects.

Less appreciated was Costin's brilliance in the realm of structural design, particularly his timber monocoque chassis for automobiles. Wood had long been used for semi-structural purposes in forming car bodies, but he was the first to use that material both to enclose the occupants and handle engine, drive train and suspension loads. As with his aerodynamic techniques, the technology for high-strength wooden structures was nothing new and, like Costin himself, had come from the aircraft industry. What made him extraordinary was that no one in the automotive world had approached either in a systematic way; it was left to Frank Costin to develop them to their logical conclusions.

Born on June 8th, 1920, Francis Albert Costin was the first of four children of an Irish/Italian mother and an English father. The young Costin had a remarkable gift for acute observation, quick analysis and a thorough understanding of abstract concepts. He also had a strong non-conformist attitude that prompted him to move in unconventional directions. Although this tendency perplexed his parents they wisely gave him free rein.

At the age of eight he decided to become an aircraft engineer, an occupation rather remote from such socially preferred disciplines as medicine, law or business. He still recalls with vivid clarity the circumstances of that event. "It was a typically English-winter's-end kind of day. I'd been bicycling through the puddles and was soaked by the time mother called me in. It was time, she said, to change clothes, to get warm and spend some time with the encyclopedia, a pastime I thoroughly enjoyed, incidentally. I sat on the window seat and paged through a random volume pausing now and again to read an interesting section. There was a northwesterly wind, with great instability in the atmosphere. The brilliant blue sky was filled with gloriously white and billowy clouds with dark gray edges, and there were intermittent showers broken by dazzling sunshine. I'd arrived at a section on aeronautics in book AA-BAC, and was fascinated by the shape of a Zeppelin gondola. Looking at it then the form of the thing was utterly beautiful. Against the backdrop of that particular day I was transfixed by the grace of the airship and inexplicably knew from that day forward I would be an aircraft engineer."

Costin's application to schoolwork reflected his goal; he mastered the sciences, particularly mathematics and physics, while reading everything he could find on airplanes, aeronautics and engineering. The shadows of World War II were on the horizon as Costin entered Harrow Weald College. He'd already formulated his own definition of an aircraft engineer: the ability to do the structural and aerodynamic design, followed by actually constructing the machine and then piloting its first flight. While college provided the former component of his definition (although much too slowly to suit him), he foresaw nothing in the curriculum to train him for the latter. In the meantime the aircraft industry was gearing up for war and begging for workers. The opportunity was too great to resist, so Costin left college and hired on with General Aircraft as a fitter. Years later, while lecturing for an engineering society, he was granted a BDIFBY (Been Doing It for Bloody Years) Degree.

After three years Costin was promoted to General Aircraft's drawing office, where the initials FAC first appeared in a small box on the right hand corner of an aircraft blueprint. Individual public recognition was neither solicited nor desired, and the industry at the time was likened to a select club, small enough for everyone to know everyone else, and with its own brand of humor and high standards of excellence. Camaraderie was enormous and the members' pride was never exhibited to outsiders. To this day Costin is a private man, partially, no doubt, as a result of these experiences. In fact, the first time he saw his name in print he came away, "all sweaty along my upper lip and feeling altogether dreadful."

By the time Germany invaded Poland Costin's love of work and sixteen hour days had accelerated his advancement as quickly as the war had stimulated the evolution of aircraft technology. Frank moved on to Airspeed, learning there about timber aircraft by means of planes like the Oxford. Assigned to the design office, he met Ron Clear, who introduced him to sailplanes. Together they formed a flying school where Clear handled the administration and Costin did the flight instruction. The fact that Frank wasn't granted his own pilot's license until 1947 didn't seem to bother anyone.

From Airspeed Costin moved to Supermarine and then to Percival Aircraft, where he was given the company's highest non-management position, that of Project Design Engineer. There he finished out the war and achieved his personal engineering goal by designing, building and flying his own sailplanes and light aircraft. Since he accomplished these projects outside company time he all but ate, slept and drank airplanes.

In 1951 Costin moved up again to become the Aerodynamic Flight Test Engineer in charge of the Experimental Department at De Havilland. The British aircraft industry was in its golden age and besides contributing to the new technology Costin was indulging himself to the fullest in what he loved best. In 1957 he was promoted to the head of De Havilland's Pure Aerodynamics Research Department. His childhood dream had taken him both to the highest and the most demanding position in his field.

Costin's love of engineering was so infectious that he was instrumental in leading others into the profession, including his brother Mike. The younger Costin came to be employed by De Havilland also, but his interests leaned more to automobiles and he spent most of his spare hours helping Colin Chapman to build the then-fledgling Lotus Company. Mike soon joined Chapman full-time and some years later formed Cosworth Engineering with Keith Duckworth. For a while it seemed that Mike's position with Lotus would never interest Frank, who believed motor cars were simply an inefficient means of surface transport. Until, that is, Colin Chapman told Mike he

*The Marcos: prototype timber chassis under construction (above). Below: views of completed prototype soon named "The Ugly Duckling" by members of British press.*

wanted an aerodynamic body on a new Lotus for the 1954 racing season.

While Chapman worked on the design of a radical space frame chassis, several men in the Lotus shop were busy drawing body shapes. One went so far as to construct a small model, but Mike noted the absence of any aerodynamic features and suggested sending it along to Frank via De Havilland's interoffice mail. After a few days Mike telephoned under the guise of finding out if the model had arrived. From the enthusiasm of his brother's voice Mike suspected that Chapman would soon have an aerodynamic body design for the Lotus Mark 8.

The diversion couldn't have been better timed. Although Costin was somewhat isolated in his position with De Havilland he perceived that the industry was changing—for the worse, in his opinion. The "Gentlemen's Club" atmosphere was being threatened by the presence of a new breed of engineer who, despite a lack of practical experience, talked in terms of cost effectiveness and production quotas. In addition, government regulations were pouring in to the extent that within ten years the aircraft industry would require as many attorneys as it would technicians to decide on design requirements. Costin was relegated to endless hours of slide-rule pushing and worse, his new position required no flying. While he thought occasionally of leaving the industry, until then he had no other direction. Perhaps, he mused, there was something to automobiles and motor racing after all.

The Lotus Mark 8 went on to become very successful, as did the rest of Costin's aerodynamic designs for Chapman. His association with Lotus lasted for three years, during which time he contracted his design work to the Vanwall F1 effort and to Maserati for a special Le Mans entry. Costin possessed an almost unbelievable capacity for work; he maintained his job at De Havilland, meaning that his work "day" usually ended at two or three o'clock the following morning. By 1958 Costin had gained sufficient recognition to leave his first love and pursue automotive design work on a full-time basis. Ironically he stayed for twenty years, the same length of time he devoted to aircraft. When he finally left it was for many of the same reasons.

## THE MARCOS

While Costin was designing sports-racing cars for Colin Chapman, he had a month's use of the prototype Lotus Seven. This model, which he accurately described as a motorbike on four wheels, was Chapman's answer to low-cost, fun motoring. Despite the Seven's impracticality it was an engaging little car and a successful clubman's racer. Costin admired its performance and handling, although he didn't like the air turbulence in the cockpit or the lack of weather protection. When it rained the water came in everywhere, including through the floor. Still, the concept of an inexpensive, small-engined, bare-bones sports car appealed to him. It should be a little more civilized than the Lotus, to be sure, but in order to derive high performance from an uncomplicated engine the car had to feature a similarly low all-up weight. The thought so intrigued Costin that he drew up a set of general specifications, but the press of other work put a temporary end to further development.

*The Marcos: rear view of revised front-end version. Note buttresses and recessed rear window. Center: revised front end on original chassis design. Below: wide chassis version which eliminated rear fenders. Opposite: 1960 Marcos GT owned by Jem Marsh.*

In 1959 Costin met Jem Marsh, the proprietor of Speedex Castings and Accessories Ltd., a modest company which manufactured and distributed performance parts for the 750 cc racing class. Inevitably their discussions came around to racing and Costin's idea for a Lotus 7 type of sports car. Marsh was delighted, because he wanted to expand his business into the specialty car field and this kind of project seemed the ideal way to begin. They agreed to pool their resources for a prototype and, if it was successful on the race track, to develop a small-scale production facility. In England at the time, racing was important to the specialty car manufacturer because it not only provided one of the best means for development and testing, but could also yield excellent publicity and a ready market for replicas. The plan was for Costin to design and build the body and chassis and determine suspension geometry while Marsh would supply the engine, drive train, suspension bits and all the trimming and hardware. Costin's decision to design and construct the complete automobile himself was quite significant, considering the fact that five years earlier he'd hardly noticed that motor cars had four wheels.

The town of Dolgellau in North Wales became Costin's manufacturing site, not because it was convenient to any motoring industry, which it wasn't, but due to his father-in-law's offer of assistance in finding suitable quarters. What greeted him was a little short of his expectations: an old, stone-walled coach house adjacent to the Lion Pub and Hotel. Fortunately a contractor's hut was also obtained so that he could endure the bitter Welsh winters. Between these two buildings Costin set to work on an automobile that would prove as peculiar as his workshops.

His first task was to lay out general specifications which conformed to the CSI's requirements for under-one-liter GT's so that the car could be homologated according to production categories. While the idea of a dual-purpose automobile is almost unthinkable today, in England at the time quite a number of brave souls drove to the track in their cars, applied numbers and went racing. Costin's goal of weather-proofing dictated a coupe configuration and, although the car was simply appointed, he saw to reasonable comfort and luggage capacity. The Lotus Seven's interior was graciously referred to as "spartan" by the motoring press, so any improvement might seem luxurious by comparison. In that the Seven also defined the intended market and the Lotus cost about $1000, Costin had to plan for extremely low manufacturing costs. Most important, the prototype had to be a winner on the race track; the success of the venture depended on it—or so Costin and Marsh thought. Unknown to either was the fact that the Lotus 7 also described what this kind of car should look like; theirs ended up a little too far out.

In selecting the type of chassis construction, Costin was faced with the engineer's dilemma: high strength versus light weight. He dismissed the small-diameter tube or space frame as too costly because of the need to tool up for both the chassis and separate body, and reckoned that a monocoque would be perfect because it combined both. Certainly a monocoque would be no easier to design, since the engine, suspension and potential impact loads had to be taken out through the skin; determining load paths and how to dissipate their energy was thus critical. Internal bulkheads formed torsion boxes which, combined with local reinforcement,

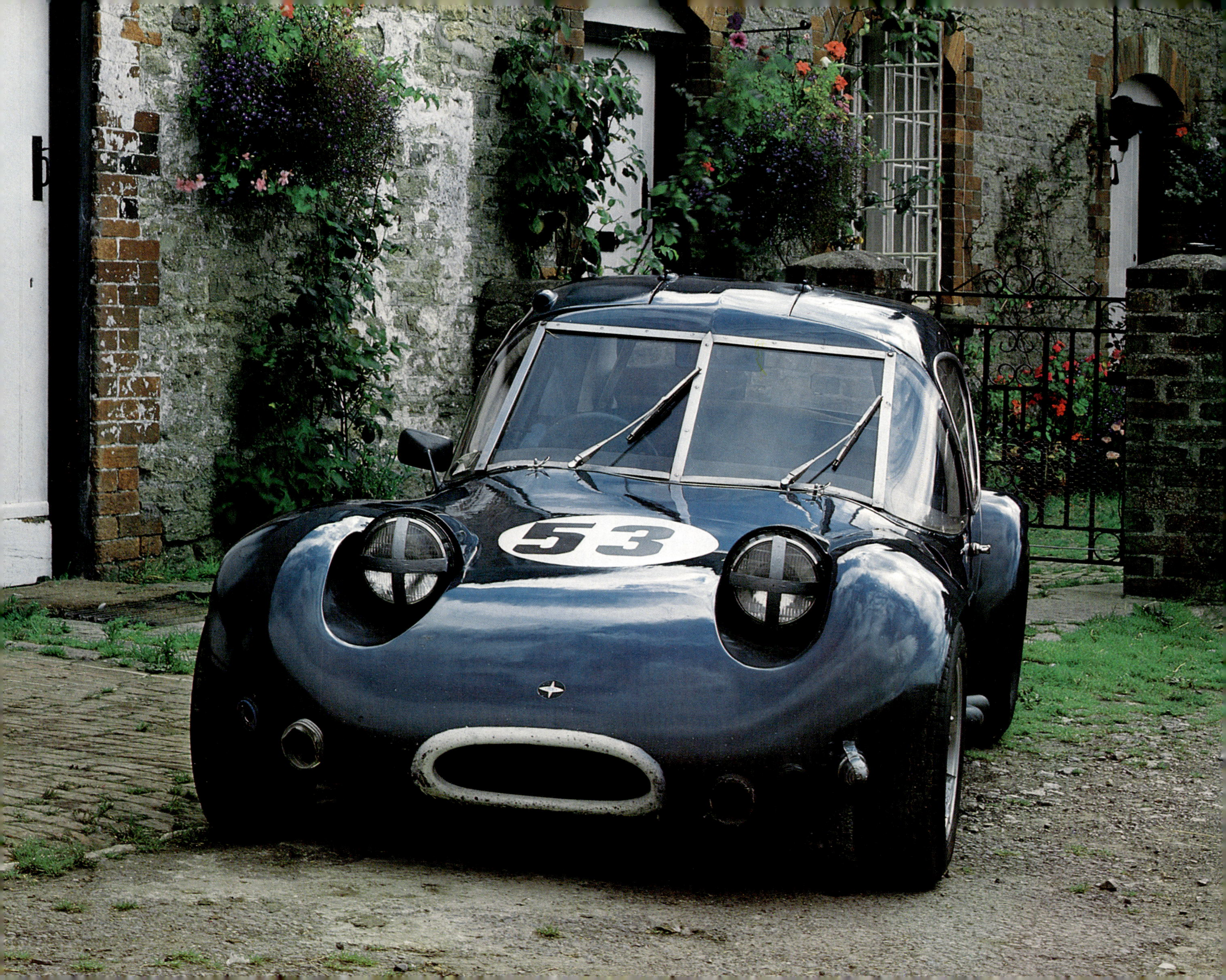
53

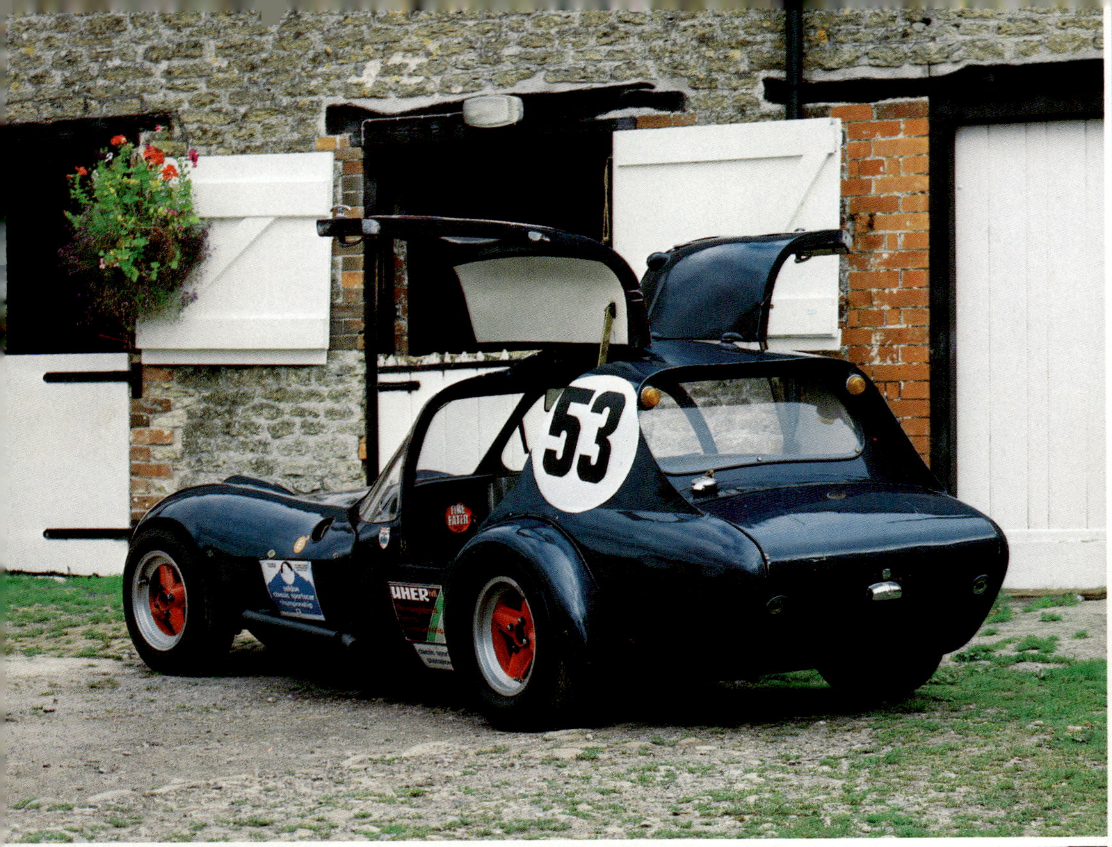
53
UHER
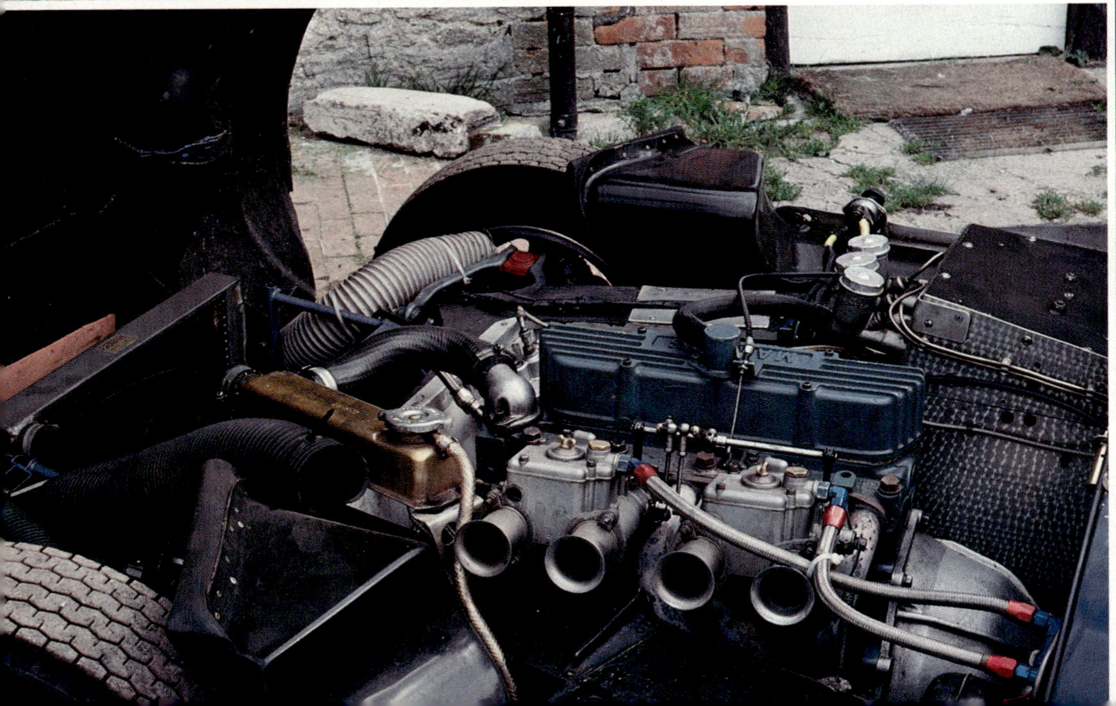
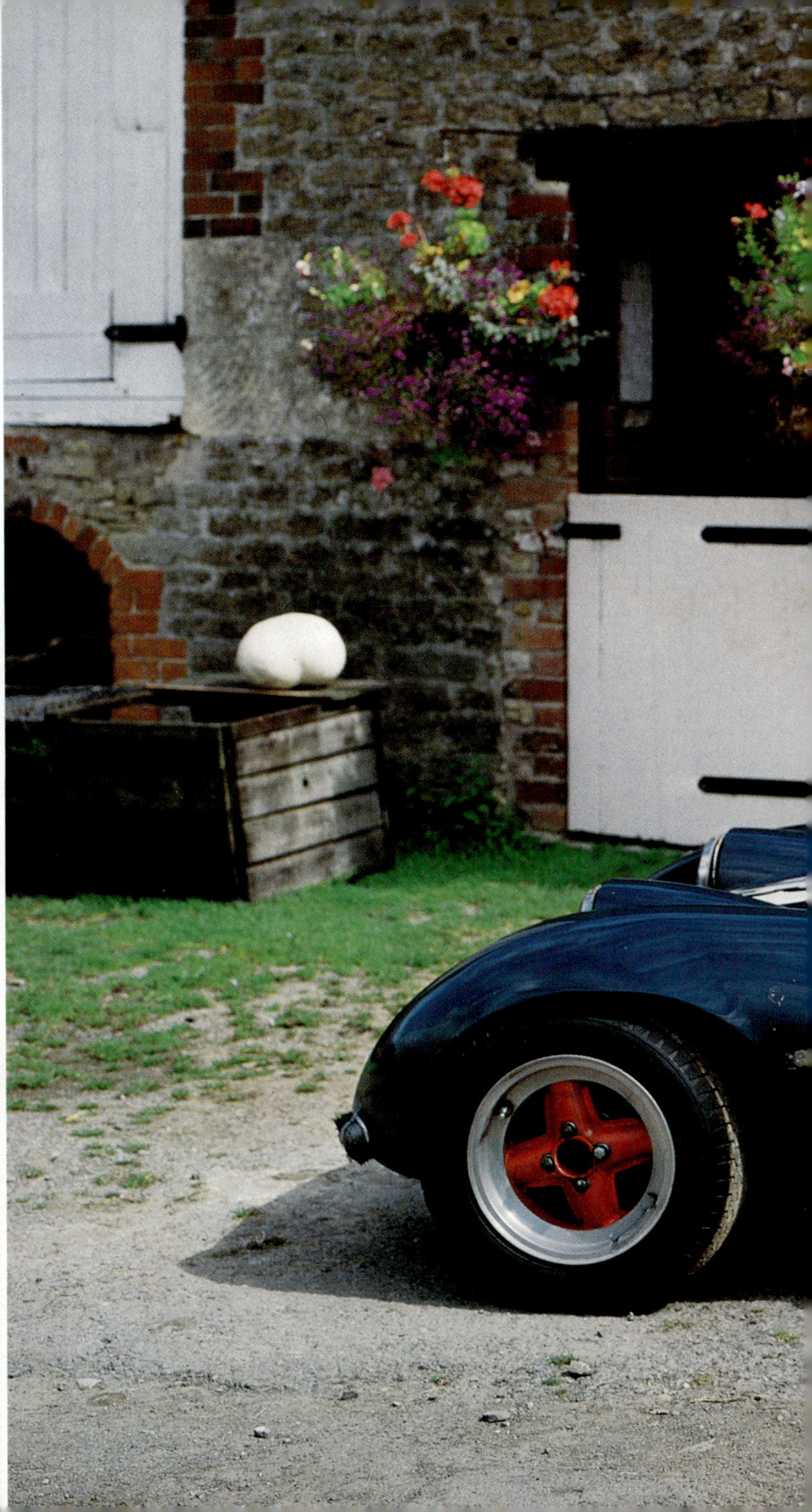

53
seldon
classic sportscar
championship
UHER hifi
Thoroughbred
Sports
Championship
1981
classic sportscar
championship

yielded the required strength for the various suspension and drive train attachment points. What stymied him was what type of material to choose. Steel was out at once due to its weight; light alloy was both expensive and far too costly to fabricate. The Lotus Elite used fiberglass for a similar body/chassis concept but, as Chapman had already learned, the technology was too new to be economical. Inevitably the process of elimination brought him to one conclusion. Incredulous as the public was likely to be, his car was going to have a timber chassis. It would be a wooden glider on wheels!

The notion of a glider was apropos because Costin had already designed, built and flown several. That fact and his aircraft background made the decision realistic because he was already familiar with the technology of wood. Marine plywoods had strength comparable to steel or aluminum when used in much thicker gauge, yet their weight was low and they were virtually fatigue-free. They wouldn't corrode, they were immune to temperature extremes and could easily be treated for fire resistance and water-proofing. Wood could even be made termite proof, although Costin never thought this was necessary. Shaping was no problem because the design called for all but a few curves in a single plane. Where compound shapes were necessary, as at the rear corners of the bodywork, they were molded out of fiberglass and bonded to the primary structure. As an added bonus to Costin's design, series production would be accomplished almost entirely in-house by an unskilled work force using simple tools. Wood made very good sense indeed.

The basic monocoque was designed around six torsion boxes; the skin consisted of marine plywood and spruce. Internal bulkheads and local reinforcement for suspension pickups and the like were constructed of top grade non-marine plywood and parana pine. All bonds were made with a synthetic resin adhesive called Aerolite which, because of excellent gap-filling properties, required minimal clamping pressure to set. Thus the production jigs were simple patterns or forms and the shapes were maintained by spring or "C" clamps.

Three torsion boxes ran fore and aft and consisted of the door sills, which utilized internal bulkheads spaced at twelve-inch intervals, and the transmission tunnel, which was strengthened by external bulkheads comprising the separate firewall and dashboard. Three additional box sections were transverse to these structures and formed the engine bay, cockpit and rear suspension housing. A fully enclosed underpanel tied everything together and curved up the sides to form the outer body skin.

Although comparable to the Lotus Elite in its use of torsion boxes, Costin's design was different in that his car's strength was concentrated below the beltline so that the top contributed little to overall rigidity. On the Lotus Elite upper-body strength was vital. When viewed without the top the design of Costin's monocoque tub strongly resembled current race car construction.

Marsh and Costin agreed early on to add insult to what they hoped would be injury by basing the shape of their car, even down to the front cycle fenders, on the Lotus Seven. Little could be done aerodynamically in this configuration, although Costin kept the nose as clean as he could. The radiator was fully ducted and, as was the practice in single-seat racing cars, the frontal air intake blended into a tapered bonnet. As was typical of Costin's designs the windscreen and its juncture with the top received considerable attention and the joint was made as smooth as possible. On the prototype a huge sheet of Plexiglas was used for the windscreen but visual distortion was so bad that it was replaced on later cars by smaller flat sections. Wool-tuft air flow testing showed that the change created little turbulence.

The top featured a design element Costin used again in later projects, a buttress-like side extension with a recessed rear window. The added surface area helped maintain smooth airflow while the window was an inexpensive but optically correct flat pane. Gull wings were chosen to ease entry over the wide door sills and to solve the problem of how to effectively hang conventional doors on a timber body/chassis. He wasn't altogether happy with this arrangement, but a more elegant solution awaited a future design.

In the interests of simplicity, aerodynamics and weight-saving the side windows were fixed in place and ventilation was handled on the prototype by means of a roof-mounted intake and exhaust duct. Later cars had a forward-located plenum chamber which fed air via hoses to eyeball-type vents on the dash, and the air was exhausted through openings above the rear window. Simply appointed yet functional, the car's interior looked very much like a light aircraft. From some angles the exterior also resembled an airplane. Most people found it undeniably ugly.

It took four months for Costin to design and build the monocoque to the point at which it was ready for installation of the suspension, engine, driveline and trim. The body/chassis weighed only 145 pounds but on test stands withstood 3000 foot-pounds per degree of twist, more than ample rigidity for racing or road use. Marsh arrived with all the parts required to finish the car, including a Ford 100E, 998 cc engine and four-speed gearbox, an Austin live axle and enough Triumph suspension pieces for Costin to use its rack-and-pinion steering and fabricate unequal-length A-arms for the front. Brakes were drums at all corners and the rear axle was located by parallel leading arms and a Panhard rod.

On the day the prototype was rolled out into the hotel courtyard and driven for the first time a name still hadn't been chosen; in their rush to complete the car for its debut neither Marsh nor Costin had given the matter any thought. But as the press date drew near the question of a name became the subject of popular conversation. Nothing sounded quite right until a member of the local town council dropped in to view the project and suggested combining Marsh and Costin to get Marcos. Despite this new name the press instantly dubbed the car "The Ugly Duckling."

While the prototype underwent road development a second Marcos was built for Bill Moss to race in one-liter GT events. During the first season he scored nine consecutive wins and captured five lap records. The Lotus Sevens were beaten handily. As a result of these successes, race drivers, including the young Jackie Stewart, ordered a few cars, but the Ugly Duckling label turned the touring customer stone cold.

At this point Marsh and Costin conferred and agreed that the timber monocoque concept was sound. The outcome of the racing program showed the structure to be completely reliable and 40,000 road miles on the prototype netted similar results. A facelift was easy enough and yielded

*The Ultimate Low-Drag Vehicle: Costin at wheel of the completed chassis; finished version showing curvature of roof. Vehicle was blue and had green-tinted windows.*

better aerodynamics. Disagreement arose when Marsh announced he wanted to change the sales plan and go after an upmarket customer. Costin, on the other hand, believed that his design was best suited to their original idea and that detail improvements alone were insufficient to attract the kind of driver who preferred to use his car primarily on the road.

While Marsh got his way the unkind reference stuck despite the better-looking front end. Even a wide chassis version which provided both increased passenger area and eliminated the separate alloy rear fenders couldn't change the label. After eleven cars were built Marsh and Costin parted company. Oddly, no financial agreement or contract was ever drawn up and the resulting problems and lure of new projects led Costin to turn Marcos Cars completely over to Jem Marsh. The marque, along with its timber monocoque, survived until the early 1970's, although it proceeded through numerous body changes in the interest of styling. By the end it used a conventional steel chassis. Marsh remained loyal to the car and today, besides operating a Marcos service and restoration business, actively participates in England's historic racing series. His skill is evidenced by a class championship in 1979 behind the wheel of one of the original Ugly Ducklings.

## THE ULTIMATE LOW-DRAG VEHICLE

Coincidental with Frank's break with Jem Marsh, he found more suitable quarters for his workshops and formed Costin Engineering Company, which solicited a wide variety of projects, not all of them automotive. Several boat-builders regarded the success of his wooden monocoque with interest, and one of his contracts was for the design and construction of two wooden pleasure craft. He kept his hand in auto racing, however, by refining the aerodynamics of a French-entered Lotus Elite for the 24 Hours of Le Mans.

Costin jumped back into the fray in 1962 when he was approached by Arnold Burton, Brian Hopton and Keith Aitchison, former financial backers of TVR cars, with a proposal to design and build a small-engined, high-performance, Grand Touring car with a very streamlined shape. Unhappy with the management policies at TVR they decided to market an automobile that would compete with that of their former colleagues. Frank was delighted because he was given complete freedom to design and build the prototype. Worried at first that his contract might include styling considerations, he was relieved to find none. Costin didn't like stylists or styling departments because they were usually unconcerned with either the engineering or the functional aspects of an automobile and believed in making aerodynamic or structural changes in the name of "eye appeal." One of Costin's maxims had long been the prayer, "Save me, oh Lord, from the statement that what looks right is right." As a result, all of his aerodynamic shapes had common origins and were derived from a blending of spatial requirements, including those for engine and drive train, occupants and suspension travel; of mathematical calculations to determine the body contours; and of an instinct derived from his aircraft experience.

For this project Costin proposed to build the "Ultimate Low-Drag Vehicle," and he was awarded £5000 ($14,000) to deliver a complete and running prototype in one year's time. The general specifications were similar to those of the Marcos, in that an under-one-liter engine was used, as was a timber monocoque, although the body was sheathed with fiberglass to provide better surface for paint. Experiments with the Marcos showed that a thin veneer of GRP (glass reinforced plastic) added negligible weight but made a world of difference in paint gloss and texture. In the interest of reduced drag to both the frontal area and cowl, heights were kept low by placing the engine at the rear. Hoped-for top speed was 85 to 90 mph with commensurate handling and brakes. Good fuel economy was expected because of the low weight and excellent aerodynamics. Costin's decision to use three-abreast seating was somewhat unconventional, but as usual his logic was good and derived from research into the average road car's payload.

Costin did his sums and put the first sketches on paper. The chassis design followed the Marcos, but with the addition of a boxed overhead surround which provided protection in the event of a roll-over. The seat was part of the monocoque's construction and consisted of a curved wooden panel which was internally braced and required only light padding and upholstery in finished trim. While the prototype had fixed controls it was planned in the production version to utilize adjustable pedals and steering column to accommodate drivers of different heights. Otherwise, the number and arrangement of the torsion box structures were the same, with some variation in the platforms and brackets for the engine and suspension mounts. All non-structural outer panels were molded in fiberglass; those not meant for removal, such as the hood and trunk lids, were bonded directly to the chassis.

The aerodynamics for the Ultimate Low-Drag Vehicle were developed by laying out the spatial parameters and then calculating mathematically pure shapes to cover them. This was done by developing parabolic contours to face the airstream and then tapering them at exactly the proper rate. As one form was laid on top of another, the fender onto the hood, for example, an expanding fillet or radius was calculated which facilitated getting the air flow back on course over the top of the car or out to the sides.

Like all of Costin's aerodynamic shapes, high-speed stability was assured by using the reverse camber principle. This meant that the mean center-line of the car's profile curved like an airfoil. Coupled with an all-enveloping undertray and a slight negative angle of incidence (the extreme forward part of the chassis was about one inch lower than the rear), the car body negated lift as speeds increased, thus remaining stable in pitch and roll attitudes. Yaw was controlled by a well-located center of pressure; this in turn was achieved by the correct amount of body-side area.

Since Costin wanted to keep the leading edge of the car as clean as possible, he put the radiator in the rear and fed it by NACA ducts. The coupe top's unusual curve was a purely structural consideration, although its effect on airflow was minimal. Because of the large expanse of fiberglass and Perspex for windows Costin wanted to avoid "oil canning"; he'd long observed that "a little decolletage usually did result in stiffness." He went after maximum visibility with liberal use of windows, including one overhead, becoming familiar in the process with the greenhouse effect and its summertime drawbacks.

Although the plan was to obtain the new SOHC Sunbeam Imp engine and gearbox, in production the prototype was powered by the more readily available 850 cc DKW motor. Drag coefficient figures were never recorded because the factory wouldn't provide Costin with horsepower numbers beyond their suggested rev limit of 5700 rpm, even though the engine was reliable to 7200. In any case, he saw 104 mph, which indicated that the Ultimate Low-Drag vehicle was slippery enough.

The prototype had several interesting features, including an aircraft-type push-pull cable for the gear linkage. All-independent suspension was used with four-wheel disc brakes, but the real surprise was that the calipers were centrally mounted magnesium castings. The central location was thought to reduce wheel-bearing loads while the exotic metal was chosen for its light weight. The front and rear uprights and wishbones were also magnesium units, all in the interest of weight-saving, with the high unit-costs figured to be amortized in a long production run.

Unfortunately, the first human transport pod, as Costin liked to call the prototype, was also the last, because of a curious turn of events. While there were problems with the car, such as cockpit ventilation and engine cooling, all of these could have been sorted out before production. What changed the plan was that TVR went bankrupt and, seeing the opportunity, the original Costin backers jumped in and assumed financial and managerial control. They had to pump their money into TVR, leaving nothing for further development of the prototype. They instructed Costin to cease work and sell the car. While this kind of end might have been disappointing to some people, to an engineer it simply meant the conclusion of another project. Besides, he had learned a great deal from the Ultimate Low-Drag Vehicle and had already made notes for the next application for his wooden monocoque.

## THE COSTIN SPORTS RACER

Costin had little doubt that his timber monocoque could handle power outputs and suspension loads far greater than were likely in his one-liter coupes, but in 1964 he was pleased nonetheless to get the chance to prove it. Still based in North Wales he met Jim Diggory, the proprietor of the local Volkswagen and Volvo dealership, who asked him to build a Group 6 Sports Racer. Diggory had raced a Marcos with success but was keen to move up to do battle with the new Lotus 23. The Lotus had shown itself to be the car to beat in both club and international events and he believed the means for doing so were better aerodynamics and lighter weight.

Construction began as soon as the lines were put on paper. Work proceeded quickly because the Sports Racer was originally meant to be a one-off; no time was spent developing jigs or tools. The chassis layout was by then familiar and the tub strongly resembled the Low-Drag Vehicle, although the boxed rollover structure was somewhat abbreviated. The seat was also similar, but in the Sports Racer it reclined to a greater degree. It was so perfectly shaped that no upholstery or padding was used, save for a pair of contoured timber blocks which provided lateral support for the driver's pelvis and lower back. Frank had done an engineering study of the human spine, and the slope of this and later timber seats was based on the results of a spine-support analysis. A departure from Costin's earlier designs was the use of sub-frames to mount the aft-positioned engine and front and rear suspension. This was done to ease accessibility and simplify maintenance, and although the concept had been used before, the execution was typically Costinian. Aircraft-type stress calculations were performed; these cleared the way for the extensive use of half-inch diameter tube and quarter-inch bolts. The triangulation and wide-spaced load paths into the monocoque were superb, but observers were startled by tubing and fasteners half the diameter they were accustomed to seeing.

The suspension was all-independent by double wishbones and the brakes were four-wheel discs that used Girling alloy calipers. A Lotus twin-cam 1600 cc engine modified by Cosworth was used; its power was transmitted through a Herland five-speed gearbox. The wheels were Lotus wobbly-web mags and the tires—at 500 x 13 in front and 600 x 13 at the rear—were supplied by Dunlop.

The Sports Racer's aerodynamic bodywork was built of light alloy by Williams and Pritchard and consisted of sections covering the front and rear subframes and a cockpit enclosure. The nose featured the usual parabolic curve, broken only by a fully ducted radiator opening. Costin's early experience with Lotus had shown that an elliptically shaped inlet was one of the least turbulence-producing in an all-enveloping front end, and this

*The Costin Sports Racer: the first model (above) nears completion; second chassis as shipped to Dr. McNamara of the U.S. The Costin Shopping Car: Costin poses with the completed prototype. Note grab handle at rear of the bodywork above lights.*

design element was by then a recognizable feature of his cars. The reverse-camber line and spatial requirements determined the car's basic profile but the joining of fender to hood shapes involved something new. In an effort to keep clean the car's leading edge as far back as possible, the fender slope began directly in front of the headlights. Although they were never fitted, Plexiglas headlight covers would have had two distinct curves joining the two shapes.

Another aerodynamic feature was that the fenders angled outward at the rear so as to accelerate air flow to the sides and over the cockpit. Instead of being completely enclosed, the top of the fender line opened at the back to exhaust radiator and brake cooling air. Designed as a single aerodynamic shape the windscreen, cockpit sides and rear deck provided minimal turbulence despite the relatively large opening. Another departure from his previous designs was the two-plane Kamm tail. Unconvinced that the Manx effect was the most effective in terms of drag reduction, Costin admitted it was the easiest and most practical solution except for the inevitably large and flat rear panel. Besides being a vibration source such a panel contributed nothing structurally until Costin hit on the idea of folding it. Voila! Rigidity without the need for internal stiffeners and their added weight.

On completion the Costin Sports racer weighed only 900 pounds, less

gas, water and oil. Initial testing by Diggory on a local race course resulted in very good impressions but the project had already consumed the bulk of his passbook account, so he decided to sell the car before committing himself more deeply to a racing program. Soon after the advertisements appeared in England's motoring magazines a check for £2000, or about $5600, arrived from what seemed to be the most unlikely of places. The buyer was Dr. Norbert McNamara, a Californian who actively raced with the San Francisco Bay Region of the SCCA. Long a fan of Costin's, he too fancied toppling the Lotus 23's dominance.

When the shipping crate containing the SR arrived, McNamara was surprised by the small diameter of the subframe tubing and fasteners but not nearly as much as were the SCCA tech inspectors. This first examination lasted over an hour. The monocoque was unusual enough but the subframes left everyone shaking his head. By enlisting all his powers of persuasion he finally convinced them to allow his car onto the race track.

Although Costin had designed sway bars for the front and rear suspension they were not installed because of the rush to ship the car. As a result of this McNamara wasn't able to stay with the Lotus 23's in the corners but once on the straight he pulled away from them convincingly. The aerodynamics were so good, for example, that he could count on a lead of six to seven car-lengths at the end of a 5000-foot straight.

The installation of sway bars proved to be a difficult task. For a time everyone who saw the car considered it too radical to fool with, until McNamara happened into Ned Bourgeault's shop. Bourgeault was a race car builder of good reputation and a fine engineer who immediately appreciated the Costin Sport Racer's advanced design principles. He agreed to add the sway bars and the test session results were so satisfying that McNamara entered the 1965 Laguna Seca Grand Prix Professional Race.

A pair of new Group 6 Brabhams were also entered and, although marginally faster than McNamara, all were practice-lapping well under the old record. When the race began one of the Brabhams tucked in behind the Sports Racer and stayed there for several laps. He finally made a move on Norbert on the uphill approach to the corkscrew turn, but made contact and McNamara slid off course. A wheel caught some soft dirt and the SR somersaulted four times. McNamara was thrown clear when his seatbelt mounts broke, and he suffered only a few cracked ribs. The mounts failed because he'd cut and rewelded them in such a way as to yield to this kind of stress. Although extemely safety-conscious, the tech inspector's skepticism had taken its toll and McNamara decided it would be better to be thrown clear rather than stay with the car in the event of a crash.

When McNamara saw the automobile after this incident he realized his mistake. All four wheels were on, nothing had broken or intruded into the cockpit, there was no movement of the steering column and the only damage was to the outer skin and the front and rear subframes. The outer torsion boxes and subframes had absorbed the impacts and, while several areas were severely damaged, all breakage stopped short of the cockpit. The crash also provided the first public evidence that the monocoque was wood. The scrutineers had never discovered that, and McNamara had been tight-lipped, fearing the car would be turned away.

More enthusiastic than ever, McNamara shot a letter off to Costin requesting another complete chassis. But since no detailed drawings had been done, Frank had to rely on his memory to build another. It took almost two years to find enough time between other projects to complete the second chassis, but McNamara was ready with a Webster-prepared Coventry Climax two-liter engine. High hopes crashed when this very expensive power plant was over-revved and ruined during the first testing session, due to an incorrect ratio in its tach drive. With a great deal of money already invested, McNamara considered the loss too great to allow him to continue in racing. He eventually got the car together and sold it to an enthusiast in Arizona. His greatest disappointment was in never achieving the SR's full potential; he insists it was one of Costin's finest designs.

## THE COSTIN SHOPPING CAR

Despite its whimsical appearance the Costin Shopping Car was a serious attempt at solving a human-factors transportation problem. The project began in response to a fad in England and on the Continent in the mid-1960's to develop a low-cost urban vehicle. Enthusiasm was so high that even the daily newspapers featured stylists' impressions of these runabouts; nevertheless, only a few people took the concept seriously. Costin, however, was one of them, and in his pragmatic way laid out what he felt were the necessary criteria of such a vehicle. Of prime importance was that it be as inexpensive to purchase as it would be to run. His calculations resulted in a two-year payment plan, based on a production run of 5000 cars, of £1.875 (about $4.50) per week. This amount also included tax, insurance and running costs based on 140 miles per week. An equally interesting specification, because a motorcycle-type gear change was planned, was that the car could be parked by an average woman lifting one end, wheelbarrow fashion, and pulling it into a parking slot. Besides the capacity for one adult the interior had to accommodate a week's worth of groceries for a family of four. Top speed was to be about 40 mph with ultra-high fuel economy but with sufficient power to climb normal road gradients. Handling was also considered and had to be in keeping with top speed. Costin also specified good weather protection along with adequate heating and cooling.

In order to qualify for lower road-tax rates the vehicle was classed as a motorcycle, which meant a maximum of three wheels. The Shopping Car had two in front and one at the rear. Pre-war Morgans had demonstrated that such an arrangement could handle very enthusiastic cornering so the reduced speeds envisioned for the Shopping Car presented no problem. Because of the proposed light weight a suspension system wasn't necessary and the axles were mounted directly to the chassis. Bicycle wheels were used, but in order to cope with increased side loads they utilized wider hubs which enabled a wide-angle lacing of the spokes. Motive power was provided by a Honda 50 motorcycle engine, while stopping ability was assured by a single disc brake on the rear wheel. One of the most common complaints made about similar vehicles was an undue sensitivity of the steering and strong feedback not unlike a go-kart. Costin designed a tiny rack-and-pinion, which not only countered these but also reduced steering effort.

The body/chassis was timber but differed from previous Costin cars in a significant reduction in the number and size of the torsion boxes and the extent of their internal bracing. To compensate for the consequent loss of strength the roof structure was stressed to contribute its own measure to overall rigidity. All this was done in the interest of weight saving, which also dictated the use of Plexiglas for the windows. The body shape was derived simply by covering all essentials, including an upright seated driver. Most of the attempts at building similar vehicles resulted in some bizarre shapes, including this one, but when Costin asked a local artist to "pretty it up" the results were disastrous. In one rendering there was no room for the driver's head or feet and the engine protruded on the side. If space was not considered a premium the vehicle ended up twice as large (and heavy) as it needed to be. In the end Costin built the Shopping Car as he'd originally designed it, although with a red paint job as one concession to pizazz.

In final trim the Shopping Car weighed only 164 pounds and Frank's wife Nan had no difficulty in picking up either end to wheel it around. Although interest in the concept waned as quickly as it began, Costin was satisfied that an absolutely basic motoring conveyance could not only be built, but could also be sold and maintained for very little money in terms of any country's standard.

*This and following page: 1967 Costin-Nathan GT owned by David Beckett*

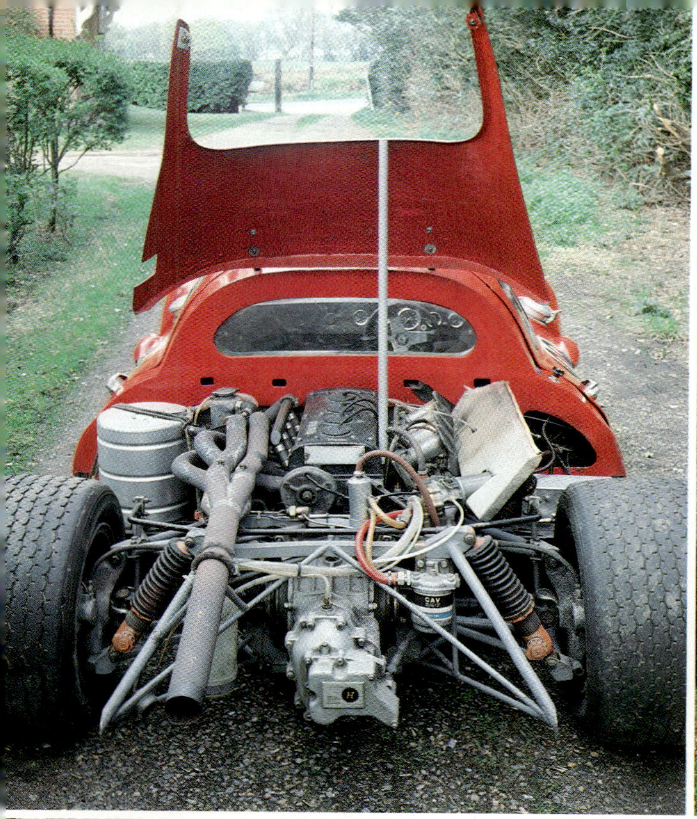

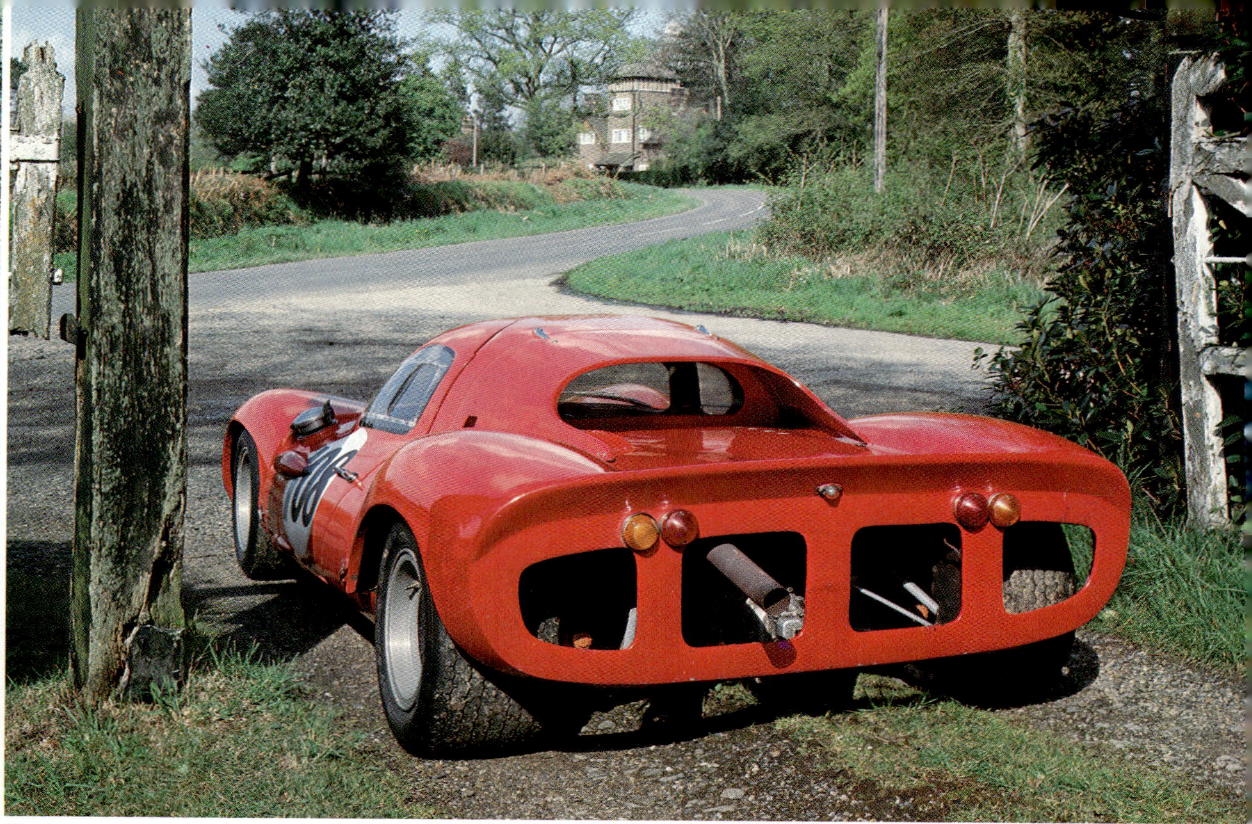

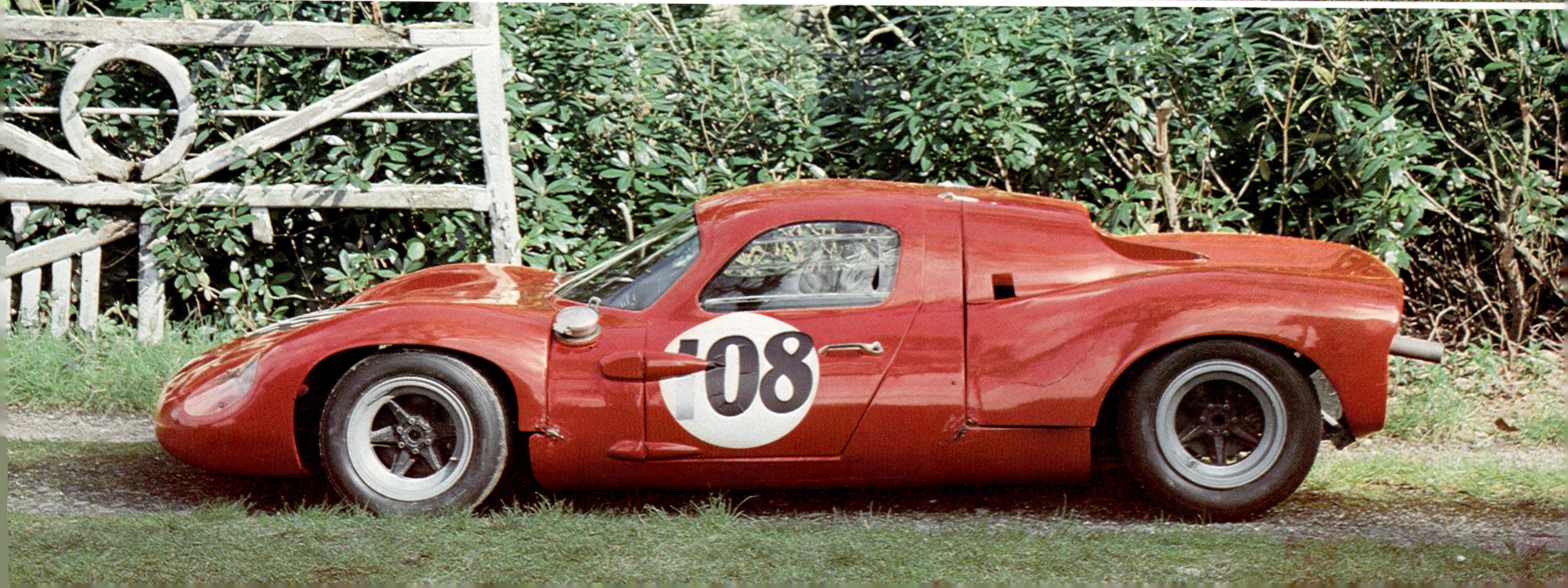
108

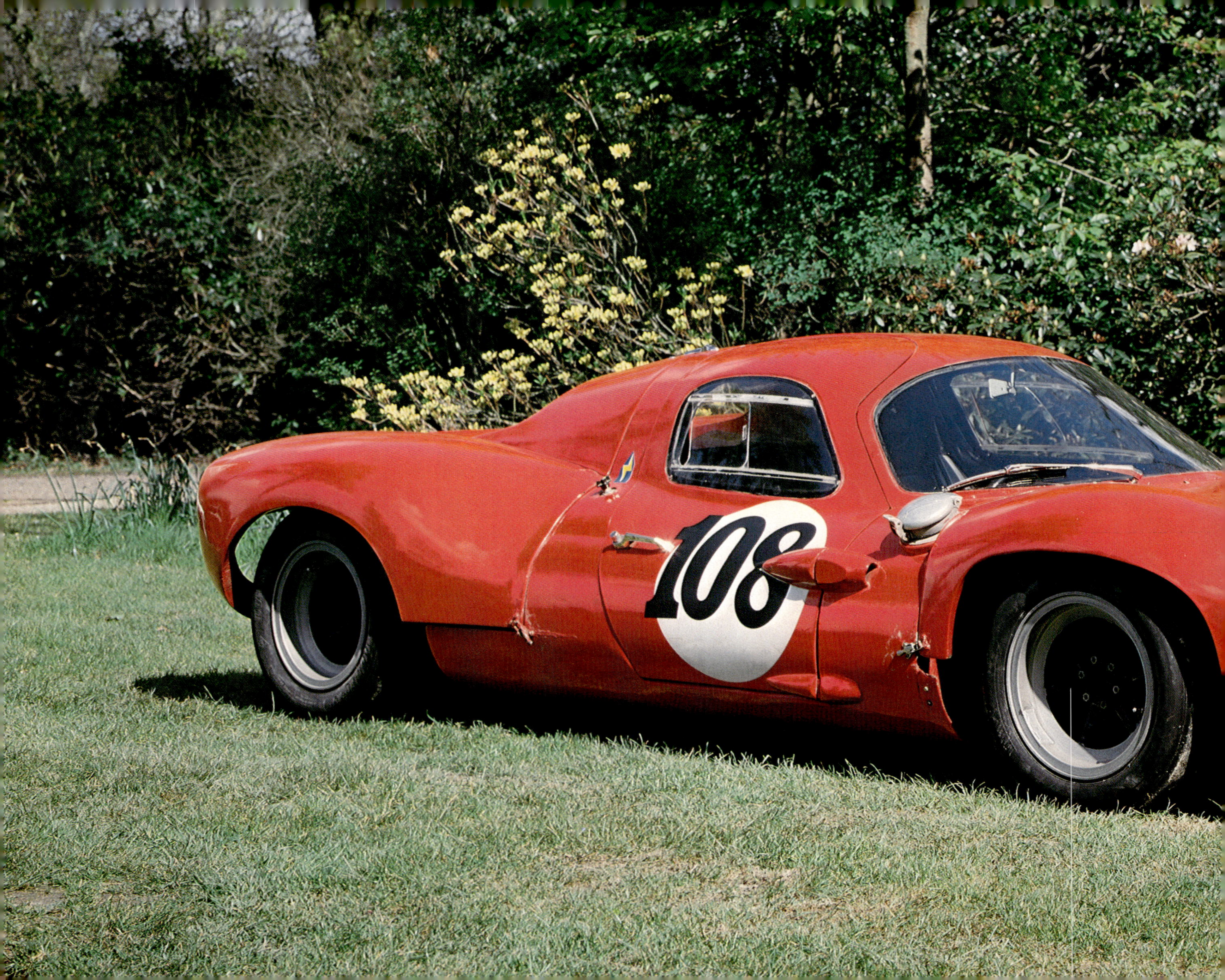
108

## THE COSTIN-NATHAN

In 1965 an engine-tuning wizard by the name of Willie Griffiths introduced Costin to the performance potential of the Sunbeam Imp SOHC motor. Griffiths was an old friend who, at the time, was works manager for Roger Nathan's London-based racing organization. Nathan was an accomplished driver who had an excellent record in a variety of cars. He campaigned one of the rear-engined Sunbeams and had just finished an extremely good year in the sedan, with numerous wins and lap records to his credit. When Costin visited the shop one day Griffiths explained the merits of the little 850 cc power plant. He extolled its alloy construction, the sophistication of the design and the resemblance to earlier, but far costlier, Coventry Climax overhead-cam engines. What grabbed Costin's attention, however, was the light weight. He could lift the 166-pound engine off the work bench and immediately got to thinking about a scaled-down version of his Sports Racer. The idea grew into a plan when Griffiths announced that he'd obtained 96 bhp from the engine bored to 1000 cc's. This, for a production motor, was nothing short of fantastic. With a Jack Knight modified Imp gearbox to allow for a rear-mounted transmission—the sedan was designed with the gears forward of the motor, in VW Beetle fashion—he could deliver a complete drive-train weighing less than 230 pounds.

Costin was really fired up over his idea for an ultra-lightweight race car and was anxious to begin its design and construction. He sketched the general layout in the usual manner and, as mentioned, patterned the timber monocoque after the Sports Racer. Roger Nathan was an early visitor who asked to race the car in return for personally underwriting the project. Costin was delighted because it seemed the perfect combination of driver and car. Further discussion provided the Costin-Nathan name and an agreement to build replicas should any racing success promote a demand for them. Although Costin wasn't anxious to tie himself to a manufacturing contract he recalled the problems McNamara had experienced and saw the wisdom in staying on at least through the development period to assist in fine-tuning the new car. He also agreed to build the jigs and tools for series manufacture as his time allowed.

The body shape followed the lead of the SR as well, although with several aerodynamic improvements. Costin raised the hood contour to reduce the transition to the fender bulge. He drew the intersecting lines of the nose and fender in front of the headlight, but on this car Plexiglas covers which incorporated the two distinct curves were fitted. The panel back of the cockpit was nearly a continuation of the cowl height and the body sides were one continuous curve. Like the SR, slots placed where the fender lines joined the body exhausted the air to the front brakes and drew in that for those at the rears. Because the car was so small and the curvature so radical, understated fins were used at the rear to increase the body side area for the control of the car's center of pressure. The slight penalty in terms of drag was offset by stability in cross-wind and cornering attitudes. A two-plane Kamm-effect form was used at the rear and the entire shape was characterized by an "all of a piece" appearance.

Tubular subframes were used front and rear to mount the engine and suspension, but Costin really "dangled out the stressing," to use his words,

*The Costin-Nathan: the prototype as it appeared at its Christmas debut for the press. Notice the duct in the rear fender and the double curvature of the headlight covers.*

and constructed it out of twenty-gauge tube. This was almost half the wall-thickness normally specified. All attachment bolts were 1/4- or 3/16-inch, which led to a response from the press and scrutineers similar to the one Dr. McNamara had received. In any event, nothing ever broke in use. The suspension was fully independent by unequal-length wishbones, and sway bars were fitted at both ends. Brakes were 9.5-inch diameter discs mounted at each wheel, with Girling alloy calipers. The wheels were 13-inch-diameter Lotus mags at 4.5 inches in width in front and 5.5 at the rear. With oil, water and one gallon of fuel the prototype weighed 860 pounds—ultra-light indeed.

A press debut was set for the Dorchester Hotel in London over the Christmas holidays and Costin enlisted the aid of his son Ron in order to finish the car on time. The prototype was painted and detailed only the day before the show, and then put on a trailer for the long haul from North Wales. They arrived a scant hour before the exhibit was set to begin. Although he'd not seen the subframes or suspension before and was as surprised as the press at their spindly appearance, Nathan was pleased with the debut. Used to fragile-looking race cars, Colin Chapman told Costin he'd nonetheless done one thing wrong—designed a pretty vehicle.

Roger Nathan took the prototype to six class wins and six lap records the following season and was so pleased he asked Costin to design a coupe for the GT racing class. The approval came quickly because a hard top would contribute greatly to what already had proved to be a very efficient shape. Called, naturally, the Costin-Nathan GT, the coupe featured conventionally opening doors, which took a surprising degree of engineering to effect. The Marcos had gull wings with hinges in the roof panel, while the Ultra Low-Drag Vehicle had doors which opened up and outward with hinges on the windscreen frame and upper body structures. Both were less than ideal from an entry viewpoint because of the need to support them either by hand or by mechanical means. Normal doors on any monocoque were problematic because, by the nature of torsion boxes, the hinges tended to be buried within the structure and were therefore inaccessible for maintenance or adjustment. The solution was an external mount which attached to a bulkhead through the outer skin. Even on a radically curved body such as the Costin-Nathan, the hinge points could thus be kept on a vertical plane so that the doors would open straight out. Costin designed cast-aluminum hinges which were faired by streamlined covers. Although drag-inducing, Frank directed some of the air to useful work by placing a duct in the upper fairing to feed air into the cockpit. The roof line featured buttresses similar to those of the Marcos. Perhaps not entirely coincidentally, this aerodynamic element was to find application by other designers, their cars including the Lotus Europa, Ferrari Dino, Pantera and Maserati Bora. Utilizing all of Costin's "state of the art" techniques, the Costin-Nathan GT coupe was an aerodynamic tour de force, and future designs would differ very little from it.

The GT was as immediately successful on the race track as the open version had been. Roger Nathan captured fourteen new lap records in 1967 and 1968 while on his way to winning both the Motoring News and Total National Grand Touring Car championships. Despite the wins and favorable exposure, sales were slow, probably due to buyer resistance to the fragile-appearing subframes and suspension. About twelve units each of the coupe and roadster were built when Costin announced that he was leaving the project. He'd begun a timber chassis for a Formula II open-wheeled race car and didn't want to be committed to supplying monocoques to Nathan, especially since the orders were sparse.

Costin assisted Nathan by providing the jigs, tools and drawings for the chassis. Unfortunately they weren't sufficient to attract another builder until Nathan approached the company that builds the famous Oxford and Cambridge University racing boats. Intrigued with the project, they agreed to build the monocoques but their price amounted to about thirty percent of the finished car—too much to be profitable—so only a few of the re-named Nathan GT's were constructed. In the end both Costin and Nathan were satisfied that the car was an excellent design that suffered from the racer-buyer's ignorance of aircraft technology. One wonders if the outcome would be different today.

## THE PROTOS FORMULA II CAR

While assisting at the exhibit of the Costin-Nathan GT at the Racing Car Show in 1966, Frank happened across Brian Hart. Hart drove formula cars for both actor Peter Sellers and Colin Chapman, and Frank had met him a few years earlier while doing some aerodynamic mods on Sellers' Formula III Lotus. He recognized Hart's enormous driving talent and the fine engineering skills he had acquired as an apprentice with his own former employer, De Havilland. Brian Hart had teamed up with Ron Harris, ex-Lotus Formula Junior and Formula 2 manager, who was eager to finance the design and construction of his own F2 car.

Harris was fascinated by the possibility of a timber monocoque single seater. After meeting Costin he instantly came up with the name Protos, which comes from the Greek work for "first," and offered Frank £20,000 to design and build four body/chassis units. One minor condition was that the car had to be on the grid for the Silverstone Formula 2 opener, then only

127 days away.

The design of the tub proceeded quickly and in theory was based on Costin's other designs. It differed in practice because of the need for a central opening the length of the chassis in which to put the driver. Torsion boxes with small openings for fluid and hydraulic lines were utilized at the extreme front and rear, but the strength in between was accomplished by circular, ring-like bulkheads surrounding the central cavity. These partitions were boxed using the outer skin as a stressed covering. Costin preferred to use a technique developed by Ferry Aviation by which mahogany strips, three millimeters (0.118 inch) thick, were placed diagonally around the chassis buck. With adhesive between the strips the entire chassis was placed in a rubber bag and a vacuum drawn. The cure took place in a low temperature oven and the result was an extremely uniform surface thickness that was immensely strong. Lack of time prevented the use of this process, so Costin relied on his old procedure of laying glued birch panels over the chassis and clamping them in place while the adhesive set. Even though the birch plys were only 3.5 millimeters (0.138 inch) thick, they lacked the uniformity of surface Frank was seeking; furthermore, the seven pounds of added weight were significant when it became necessary to save ounces to bring the car in at under the maximum allowable weight.

One of Costin's greatest interests had been the study of automobile safety, and he'd written several technical papers on the subject. One of his strong concerns was fire, which led him to incorporate an unusual philosophy into the design of Protos' side-mounted fuel tanks: that they should break away in the event of a crash. The tanks were light alloy with Neoprene covers and were held in the chassis by narrow section side ribs.

The front suspension featured a conventional rack-and-pinion steering and a kind of double-wishbone system. The lower member was made of elliptical rather than round tube for drag reduction; it utilized wide-spaced pickups to spread the loads into the chassis. The top member was V-shaped, with the inner section set far forward in the nose in order to actuate inboard springs which had to clear the driver's foot-box. The outboard part of the V was swept backwards to achieve the wheelbase Costin wanted relative to the center of gravity. This ingenious configuration was ultimately changed to a true wishbone because of brake judder, which could be traced to play in the spherical rod ends magnified by the length of the non-triangulated arm.

Front and rear uprights were monocoque structures made of magnesium. This was accomplished by casting the pieces in channel form and then welding on covers to close the openings. In order to reduce angularity change in the rear suspension, Costin specified very long halfshafts which were fabricated from Lancia parts. At 19.5 inches in length they certainly looked radical but none ever broke.

The rear suspension was again a kind of double wishbone arrangement, except that three top arms were used and two of them were parallel. This was necessary because the half-shafts were closer to the upper arms than the lower and the resulting chassis loads had to be taken out over a very wide area. A tubular subframe was bolted to the rear of the chassis to carry the Cosworth engine and suspension members, and Costin continued his practice of using highly stressed thin wall tube and small diameter fasteners.

*The Protos Formula II Car: fifth scale model (top). Center (left): Selfridge's Department Store debut. Note bubble canopy, front suspension, diameter of rear suspension members. Right: front view of Protos chassis under construction, showing side ribs, designed to shear on impact, for holding fuel tanks in place. Bottom: Brian Hart's Protos following Lotus. Note Protos' "clean" appearance when compared to that of the Lotus.*

While outsiders found the timber monocoque controversial, the body shape was considered sensational. All of the design elements were familiar Costin techniques, from the elliptical air intake to the two-plane Kamm rear end. What startled most people was the bubble windscreen meant to eliminate turbulence created by the driver's head. Even though this windscreen eventually had to be slotted to improve the visibility of a surface quickly splattered with oil and debris, the effect on airflow was negligible. In comparison to the Protos' contemporaries the car was remarkably free of drag-inducing excrescences.

With Costin and Hart logging twenty-hour work days and thousands of miles chasing parts, the Protos was made ready for its press debut at Selfridge's Department Store in London, held a few days before the F2 season's opening race. One of the first testing sessions at Snetterton provided both their first disappointment and Costin's realization that wood might not be ideally suited to the high technology of single-seat racing cars. The Protos weighed in at seventy pounds over the minimum limit. After the first few races it also became apparent that the car would never attain the ultimate cornering power of top-level competitive machines, because Costin had positioned the fuel tanks too high in the chassis and the center of gravity ended up three quarters of an inch above the ideal. This was maddening considering that, in a straight line, nothing could touch the Protos. Brian Hart, Pedro Rodriguez and Eric Offenstadt drove for the Protos Team and all experienced the same frustration of being able to streak away from the opposition on the straights only to lose the advantages in the corners. As evidence of the car's potential on high-speed circuits, Brian Hart's Protos held the lap record at Hockenheim from 1967 to 1969—a remarkably long span in Formula II racing.

Pedro Rodriguez was the driver who put the Protos to the ultimate test at the Enna circuit in Sicily. While dicing with the leading Matras he was cut off in a high-speed corner and then shunted a track-side barrier. Both fuel tanks peeled away at the point of first impact but Rodriguez continued a monumental slide, bouncing wildly off the Armco lining the circuit. After finally coming to rest he climbed out, suffering nothing more serious than minor bruises, and unaware that pieces of his car were seen floating in the infield lake.

Although Hart and Costin believed a Mark II version could be made competitive by correcting the center of gravity and pairing off a few pounds, Ron Harris lost interest in the project even before the first season was completed and abandoned the team. Without financing there was no possibility of further development or redesign, so the cars were sold off to cover the remaining debts and the team disbanded. Costin was disappointed that the Protos wasn't a winner the first time out, not for his own sake but for Brian Hart's. He had grown to admire him enormously and believed he had the makings of a Grand Prix champion.

## THE AMIGO

Clearly, the 1960's was a special decade for motoring enthusiasts in England. Favorable conditions supported both Costin and dozens of other specialty car manufacturers, kit car builders, fiberglass body constructors

**1972/80 Costin Amigo owned by Nick Costin**

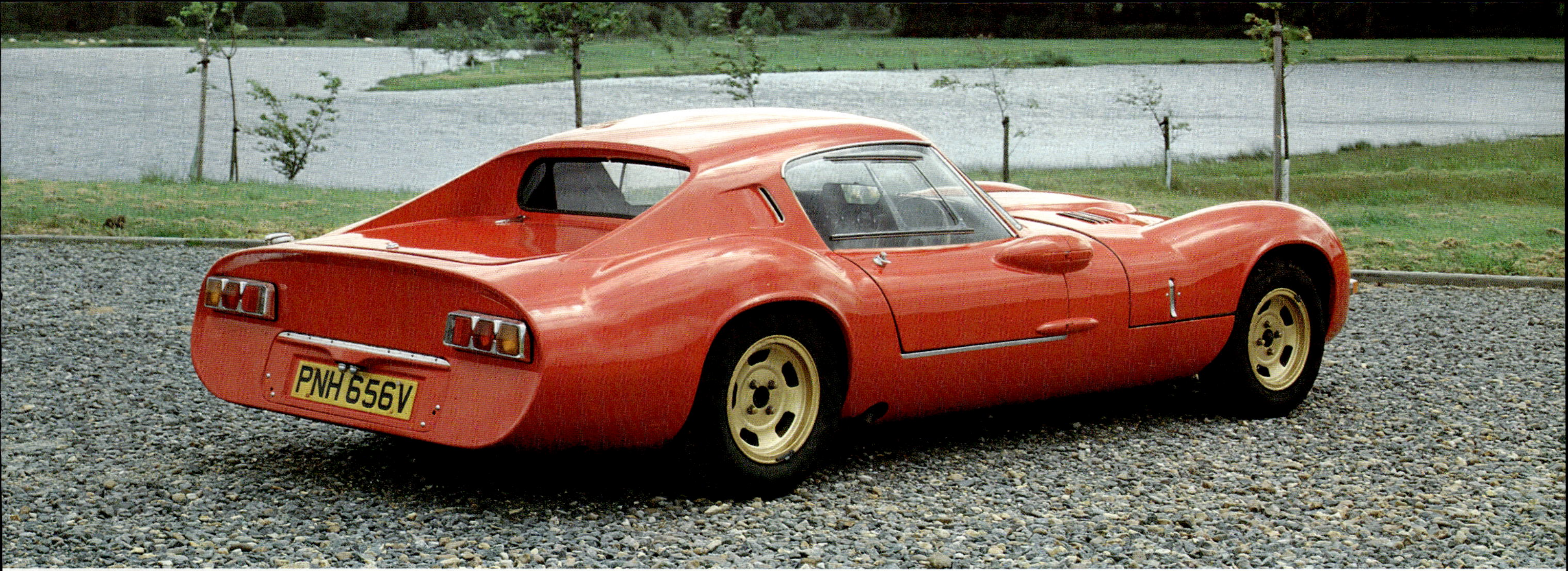
PNH 656V

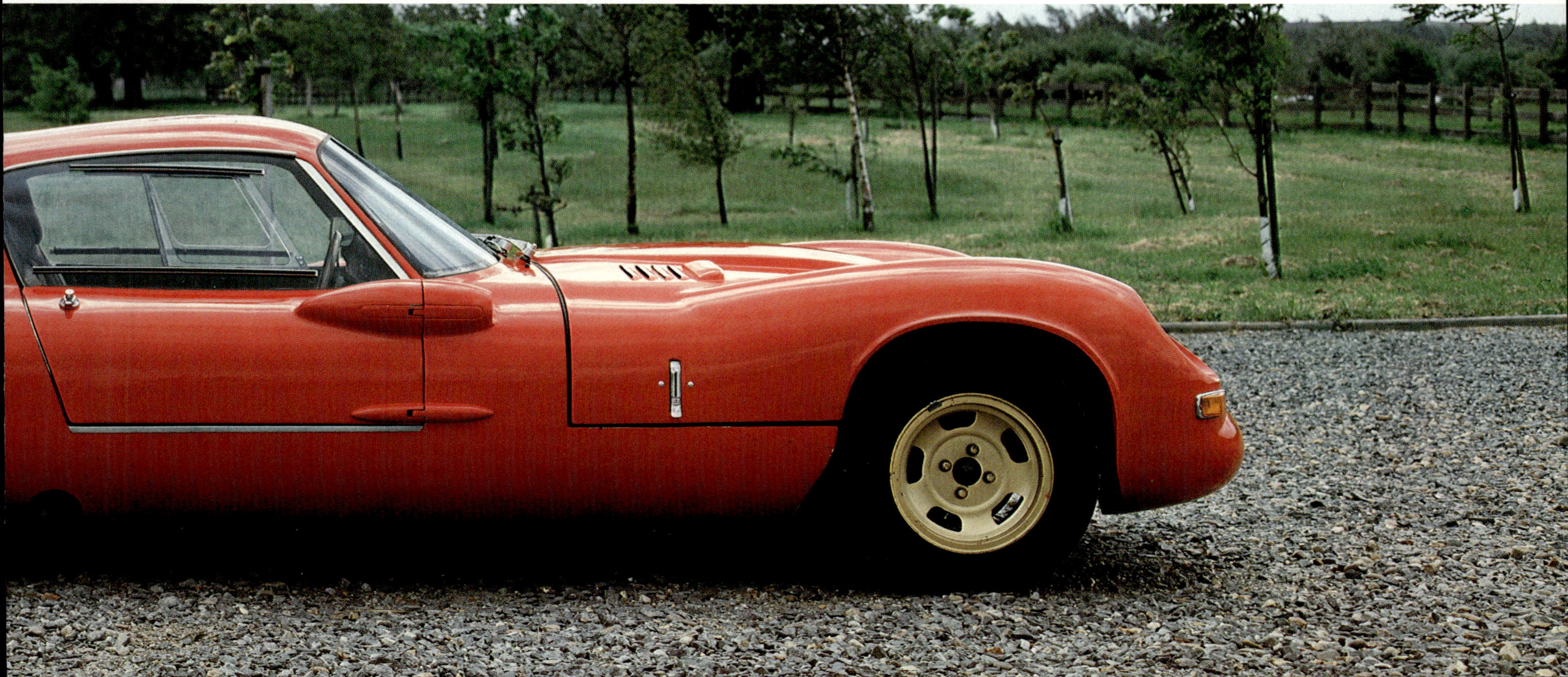

and the like. Oil was cheap, government restrictions were few and there seemed to be ample money for new projects. Frank was able to begin several of his designs secure in the knowledge that someone was already looking for his address to offer financial backing. In many respects the climate resembled Costin's time in the aircraft industry, but as the decade drew to a close he foresaw a similar end. The days of the private entrepreneur or patron with sufficient capital to finance independent automobile designers and constructors, no matter how brilliant, were almost over.

The Value Added Tax and the first oil crisis were coming, and easy money was getting scarce. In Costin's view there was also a shift in the automotive industry away from organic and therefore potentially aerodynamic designs toward angular and pie-shaped bodies. These required lips, spoilers and dams just to achieve acceptable levels of control; there was little chance of achieving anything superior. This, of course, did nothing to change his mind about stylists or those who mindlessly followed their dictates. Nevertheless, Costin was convinced that there had to exist a more sophisticated clientele that would welcome the opportunity to own a car built around advanced engineering principles and incorporating the best in aerodynamics. He envisaged a fast but proper grand touring car, one which offered all of the normal amenities while asking the fewest compromises from the driver. But for a few outside contracts and a consultancy or two, this project was his final attempt at automotive design and manufacture. It was also the culmination of everything he'd learned and most of his automotive aspirations.

Costin's general specifications for the GT included the ability to cruise at 100 mph at less than 5000 rpm. According to the space he allotted for fuel a range of 250 miles per tank of gasoline was assumed, calling for fuel consumption of around 30 miles per gallon. The engine was a proprietary unit chosen for its reliability and ease of service. Luggage space, driver comfort in terms of heating, ventilation, seating refinements and the arrangement of controls were determined with long distance travel and the need to eliminate fatigue in mind. Safety was also specified by continuing with the timber monocoque and its deformable crash barriers. In addition to this, Costin designed a rollover bar, breakaway fuel cell and a suspension system which yielded neutral handling characteristics. Low weight and an excellent top speed were not detailed in promotional material, but assured. Even the name was chosen to elicit good feelings: "Amigo, the friendly car." The trouble was that Costin took on a partner and backer, Paul Pyecroft, who believed that the deluxe specification demanded a premium price; the cognoscenti also had to be well heeled.

The chassis was similar to Costin's previous designs except in the placement of the engine and the need to accommodate "structural air" for the rear suspension. Although mid-engined by definition, the Amigo's motor was ahead of the driver and called for a substantial torsion box which formed the cowl. In addition to this, outriggers extended the chassis sides forward of the firewall because the engine was mounted directly to the monocoque, albeit through suitably reinforced timber brackets. The rear suspension required a large transverse box section to give room for long parallel leading links. The added torsion boxes were immensely strong because of the internal bulkheads, but they also contributed to the overall length, which ended up at thirteen feet seven inches. For a pure two-seater the Amigo was a long car. It was also low at three feet six inches, prompting Costin to design an extraordinary optional accessory, the visual warning indicator. This was a flashing light set atop a streamlined pylon on the Amigo's roof, enabling traffic to see the car over hedgerows. It was also a slick way to conceal the radio antenna.

*The Amigo: Costin with developmental prototypes. Car on left has visual indicator, roof-top scoops and front radiator airfoil. One at right has NACA duct-to-feed carburetor and forward-facing scoops for heater plenum.*

Like the Low-Drag Vehicle the chassis' exterior surfaces were covered with a thin fiberglass veneer. This material was also used for the hood, trunk lid and coupe top. A steel hoop was imbedded in the windshield surround for added rigidity and rollover protection, although the latter safety feature was handled primarily by a triangulated steel roll bar built into the rear roof structure. The body shape reflected pure Costinian aerodynamics, from the reverse camber line to the nose and tail treatments. While the elements had been used before and the family resemblance was unmistakable, the Amigo nonetheless had a look all its own.

Costin chose the Vauxhall Victor as his source for engine, drive-train and major suspension components. This came as a surprise to many, in that Vauxhall's image was decidedly non-sporting. Nevertheless, the components were robust and reliable and could be serviced in England by an extensive dealer network. At two liters (later increased by the factory to 2.3), the Victor's SOHC four cylinder engine was very lightly stressed and produced 100 bhp at 5800 rpm with good torque characteristics and reasonable smoothness.

The gearbox featured an overdrive on third and top gear and, with the 3.9 differential and standard limited slip, the Amigo did 0 to 60 in 7.5 seconds and had a top speed of 137 miles per hour. Fuel economy worked out to almost exactly 30 mph with a large measure of credit going to the car's aerodynamics and 1450 pound curb weight. A curious-looking exhaust manifold was provided by Vauxhall; it was cast in reverse so the flow ran forward relative to the engine. This was done so that the exhaust pipes and mufflers could be placed inside the door sill torsion boxes to exhaust through openings just forward of the rear wheels. The purpose of this unusual arrangement was to maintain an undertray devoid of any projections that would disturb the airflow. In fact, the only disruptions to the smooth underside were the access and drain holes for the engine, gearbox and differential and an inlet for the heating and ventilation plenum.

A steel tube subframe was placed ahead of the engine to support the radiator and front suspension. Victor top and bottom wishbones were used, but Costin added an adjustable trailing arm to widen their base. Front brakes were discs, also from Victor, but the springs were uprated and coiled over Koni shocks. The rear suspension utilized the Victor rear axle and drum brakes. Location was provided by parallel leading links and a Panhard rod. Uprated springs with Konis were used here also but the shocks were the very sophisticated self-leveling type.

The Amigo fairly bristled with welcome and sometimes novel touches. For example, all the windshields were tinted along the top, and twin shoulder harnesses and lap belts were standard. A lidded hatch at the lower rear body panel housed the spare tire, while another in the right rear flank contained the jack and a wheel chock. The trunk lid featured a drop-down tray, which revealed a set of tools, and the interior and trunk compartments were fully carpeted.

As the first prototypes rolled off the "production line," several variations occurred as Costin tried out new ideas. As in the Costin-Nathan, the upper door hinge fairings incorporated fresh air inlets. A few cars had scoops mounted on the roof for additional cockpit ventilation, although they were soon eliminated as being unsightly. A better device was the cable-operated airfoil in the radiator intake, which could be rotated in order to blank off incoming air to quicken engine warmup or maintain optimum running temperatures in very cold weather. At least one Amigo had the minor instruments set in a console mounted aircraft-fashion above the windshield, while the others had them lined up on the dash but angled towards the driver. Even though more sophisticated than the Marcos, an aircraft "feel" characterized the inside of the Amigo, a quality admired by some road testers and criticized by others. Everyone, on the other hand, appreciated the extensive owner's handbook, even though a few wondered at the significance of its "Pilot's Instructions" title.

To a man, the motoring journalists marveled at the comfort and deceptive ease with which the car achieved and maintained high cruising speeds. They remarked at the absence of wind, road and mechanical noise and at the solid feel of the car. Handling was praised as well, with a few testers placing it in the Lotus Elan class. As with their compliments, however, their criticisms were universally echoed. No one liked the sliding glass windows, the difficulty of getting into the car through smallish doors or the chore of fastening the belts and harness. Some found visibility to the rear a problem, while others complained of limited foot room. What really caused them all to gasp was the price. At £3300 (about $8,000), the 1972 Amigo was set for battle with such heady and well-established companies as Jaguar, Porsche and Lotus. Somehow a car with a wooden chassis just didn't have the same connotation.

But the Amigo never really got the chance to prove itself. With only seven on the road, some of them developmental prototypes, Pyecroft decided he'd had enough of being an entrepreneur and relinquished the company to Costin. Pyecroft had been very effective in handling the business side of the project, including setting up sources of component supply, locating a small factory building for the production line, doing the publicity and the hundreds of other time-consuming jobs necessary in getting a limited-production car company off the ground. His problem was in finding sufficient time to maintain the commitment. Pyecroft's help had been vital to Costin because it left him free to design, build, test and refine his Amigo—in other words, to indulge himself in the way he liked best.

Although several backers came forward, all wanted Costin to head the company since none had the inclination to take over the organizational duties. Predictably, Frank declined their offer, having no desire to trade his drawing table for a paneled office. The stalemate ended in receivership, and all the cars, including two uncompleted chassis, were sold off to cover expenses.

## AFTER THE AMIGO

That the Amigo was much more than an interesting concept and really did appeal to specialists was evidenced by the fact that a steady flow of inquiries persisted. As recently as 1980 Costin answered questions from potential backers on reviving the project. Of course, aerodynamics and light weight have taken on renewed importance in a world hard pressed for energy, and a chassis constructed out of a renewable natural resource may no longer be regarded as merely novel. But Costin's reluctance to accept offers for financial support continued. No one, it seemed, was willing to offer the other commodity that he required most, the freedom to leave the project at the appropriate time in order to get on with the new ideas that constantly spilled off his drawing board.

When the dust finally settled on the Amigo in 1972, Frank moved to Kettering and set up Costin Research and Development Company. His first priority was to develop some of the non-automotive ideas that had long taken a back seat to his cars. One of these was based on the contoured timber seat he used on the Sports Racer, Costin-Nathan and Amigo. Costin shaped an orthopedically correct chair for home use and molded it out of fiberglass. Another unusual project was that undertaken for Joe Bamford, a director of JLB, heavy equipment builders. A dedicated yachtsman, Bamford asked Costin to reduce the drag on the hull of his 128-foot, 250-ton Romantica. "Wasn't fast enough," he said. The result was a curious-looking appendage stuck on the bow; the tests showed that hull resistance was cut by nearly twenty-five percent.

Costin's next inquiry came from the March Formula I Team. He designed the bodywork on the Type 711, which was characterized by its "tea table" front airfoil and parabolic nose. While the engine and chassis were marginally competitive, Costin reckoned he picked up 60 to 70 brake horsepower on the aerodynamics alone.

Another project came from his old friends at Vauxhall Motors. Even though close ties were forged during the Amigo days, Frank was somewhat surprised to be asked to assist in their racing program. Even though Vauxhall was part of General Motors United Kingdom it observed the stateside ban on racing, at least officially. Not wanting Ford (UK) to grab all

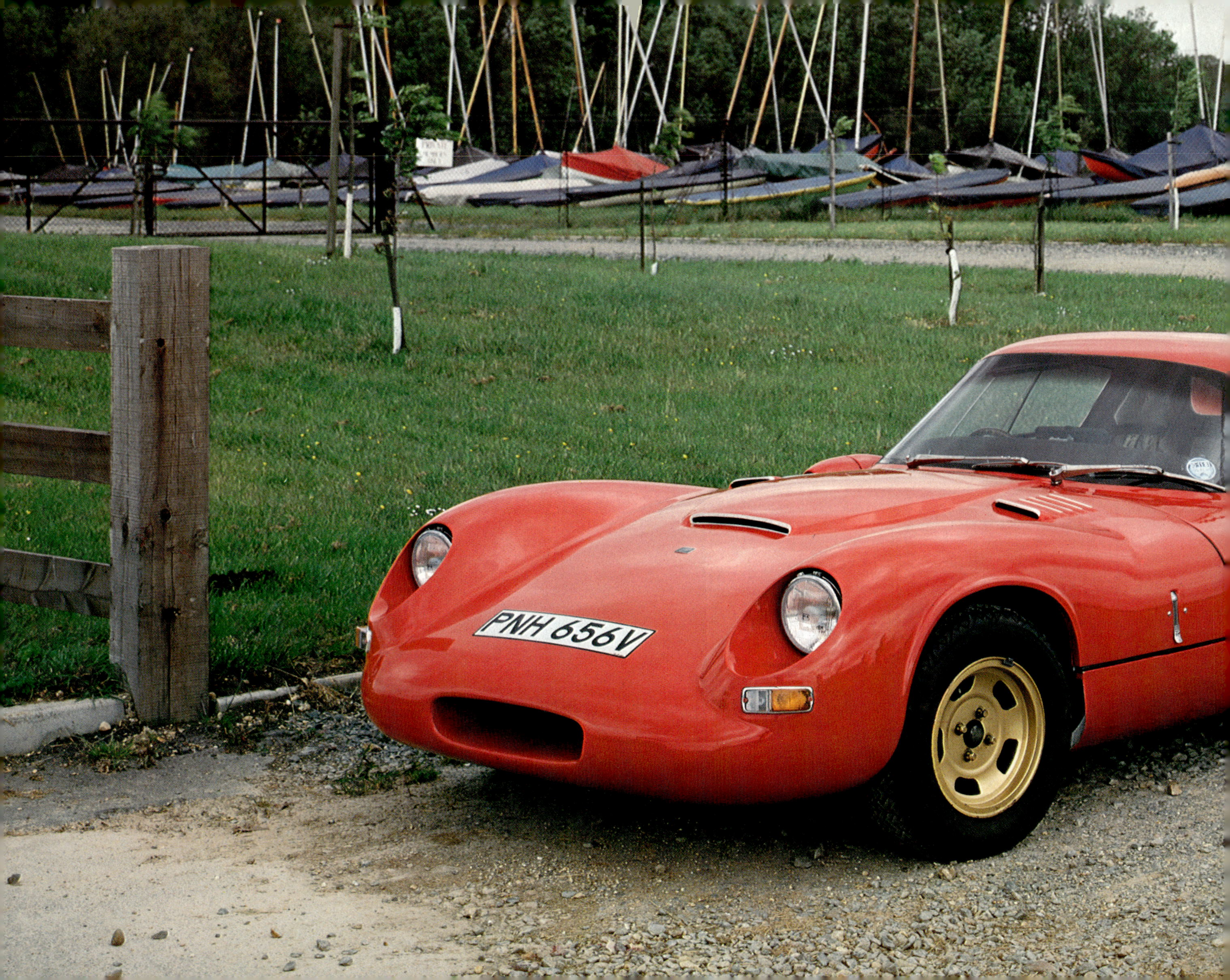
PNH 656V

the motorsport headlines, however, Vauxhall smiled down on a group of enthusiastic dealers that called itself Dealer Team Vauxhall.

Bill Blydenstein, high performance and rally specialist, provided the team's organization and shops. The plan was to field a Vauxhall sedan in the new Super Saloon class. In 1973 DTV ran a Ventora, which was destroyed in a crash, and in 1974 a Firenza; they were nicknamed Big Bertha and Baby Bertha, respectively. Both used a 496 horsepower Repco modified V-8. The wheels were the widest available at the time, twelve inches in front and fifteen at the rear. Costin designed the suspension and subframe systems and made provision for detail aerodynamics, such as the flush fit of the windscreen and side window glass, the removal of all drag-inducing bits like the rain gutters and the subtle rounding of front body contours. Unfortunately, Vauxhall's styling department insisted on making the cars look like racers and adopted such trendy go-fast devices as a front air dam.

The sedans were spectacular and highly successful. Gerry Marshall drove for the Team and his 250 pound frame was matched by an equally proportioned sense of humor and extremely skillful sideways style of driving. Numerous wins and lap records fell to Dealer Team Vauxhall and in 1976 so did the Championship.

Meanwhile, Costin's prediction was coming to pass, and the automotive industry changed. Despite the first oil crisis and its foreshadowing of things to come, fashion decreed the end of organic shapes and Costin's popularity waned. As in the aircraft business twenty years before, well-meaning legislation had the effect of slowing the advancement of technology. Frank knew it was time to move on.

He felt the need to lay out one more set of specifications, though, for the Ultimate Economy Car. Although constructed only in scale model, his calculations indicated a thousand pound curb weight. It would have been remarkably light considering its proposed size, at 12 feet 4 inches in length, 64 inches in width and 47 inches in height. As with the Low-Drag Vehicle, seating was three abreast but the specifications allowed for males six feet tall. Ample luggage space and all the normal touring amenities were also provided.

The engine was placed behind the cockpit and allowance was made for a displacement range from 600 cc to one liter. Even with the larger powerplant, fuel economy was calculated at 40 to 50 mph, with a top speed of 100 mph. Again, light weight, cleverness in structural design and excellent aerodynamics made all the difference.

With that, Costin closed shop and moved to the south of Ireland. He'd been approached by several young engineering firms to join their boards of directors, to assist in the development of their product lines and to train new engineers. Costin had envisaged such a future for himself for several years. Specialized industry was relatively new to Ireland and the Government set up numerous concessions to encourage its growth. That and a beautiful seacoast ideal for sailing was all the encouragement he needed.

Frank Costin has since worked on a variety of projects, from wind-driven generators to undersea exploration devices, but in 1981 something suspicious appeared. Costin designed the suspension system for an airport firetender which, during figure-eight testing on the runways, was reported to handle like a sports car. ♧

*1972/80 Costin Amigo owned by Nick Costin*

# The Golden Age

1911 Renault CF Limousine ❧ Owner: Crawford Auto-Aviation Museum

*By Paul Brennan w*

# THE LUXURY CAR

*1928 Hispano-Suiza H6B Cabriolet de Ville ❧ Owner: Morton Y. Bullock*

*Photography by Roy Query*

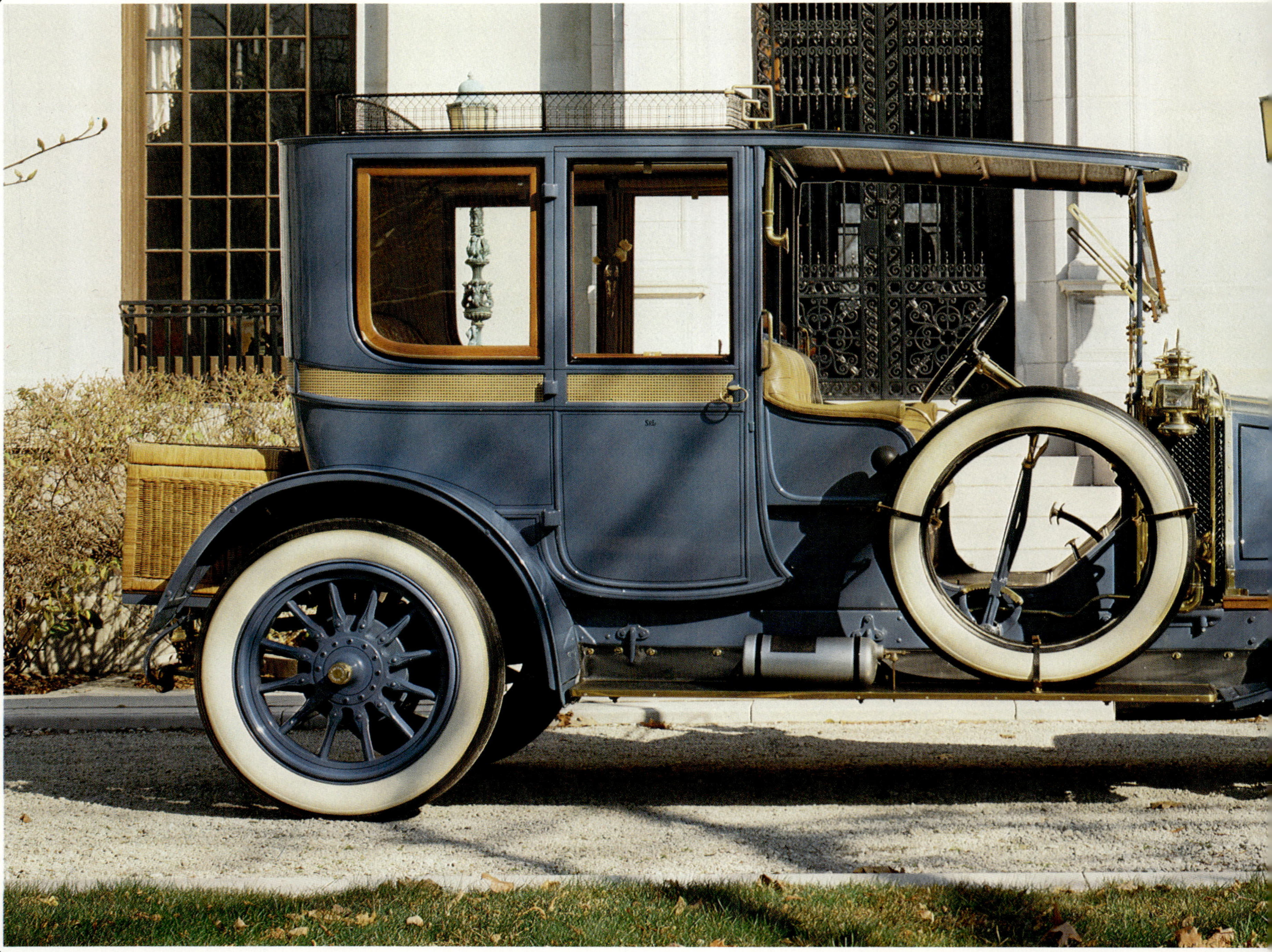

Most authorities agree that the Golden Age of the formal luxury automobile extended from about 1909 to about 1914 and continued, after the interruption of the First World War, to 1932, when the Depression called a halt to most custom coachbuilding in the United States and Europe.

The consensus stops there. Anyone who makes even a cursory examination of the literature devoted to custom-built luxury automobiles can find a number of fine, detailed articles and monographs about an individual prestige chassis or single coachbuilder. But the body of more comprehensive studies is small and self-contradictory, and there is virtually nothing that gives a systematic overview and analysis of the luxury car phenomenon itself.

Indeed, there is chaos even in a matter as elementary as the definition of the two basic types of formal car, the limousine and the town car. Most purists define a limousine as a chauffeur-driven automobile that is sectioned for privacy by a glass partition between the driver and passengers. The driver is protected from the elements by a permanent roof and, at the sides, by curtains or windows. By contrast, a town car is a chauffeur-driven automobile used within a limited geographic range for business or personal transportation. The chauffeur is not formally isolated by a barrier, and the degree of protection given to him varies, depending on the coachmaker and model year. (See AUTOMOBILE *Quarterly*, Volume IV, Number 1.) But these definitions have never been consistently observed, whether by customers, journalists, automobile historians or coachbuilders themselves. Some writers use the terms interchangeably. The noted designer Hermann C. Brunn, on the other hand, suggests the existence of a great chasm between the two body types when he writes: "To own a town car signified not only that a man was wealthy but that he also appreciated the aesthetic things of life. The same glamour was never attached to the limousine."

If there is considerable confusion about the history and terminology of formal coachbuilding, there are at least a few questions and concerns that recur, both in contemporary and retrospective works. Sometimes these questions are stated overtly; at other times they are implicit. But whether we pick up a number of *The Horseless Age* from 1909 or an issue of the *S.A.E. Journal* that was published at the end of the era, in 1930, the same themes appear. What was the proper relationship between the luxury automobile and the formal carriage of the Nineteenth Century? Should designers and fabricators concentrate on assembling an array of finely finished details, or ought they to think first of the car's overall lines? What were the advantages of a light as opposed to a heavy luxury car? And what were the pros and cons—aside from the obvious financial ones—of limited production?

One way to discuss the way in which the builders of luxury automobiles addressed these issues is to look in some detail at two representative cars of the period, one built before World War I, the other built after the Armistice. For this purpose we have selected a 1911 Renault CF limousine bodied by Brewster and a 1928 Hispano-Suiza bodied by Hibbard & Darrin.

For those of us who think, at the mention of Renault, of Le Car, Paris taxicabs or the flagrantly abused roadster in which F. Scott Fitzgerald and Ernest Hemingway traveled north from Lyons with reserves of truffled chicken and Mâcon, it might come as a surprise to hear that Renault was an exporter of a sizable number of large luxury chassis during the first third of the Twentieth Century. In fact, one Renault six-cylinder model, with a wheelbase of 157 inches, was the largest chassis to be shipped out of Europe during the Twenties.

As Patrick Fridenson and Anthony Rhodes have pointed out in their commercial histories of Renault, Louis Renault was sufficiently impressed by the dire financial consequences for France of the Panic of 1907 to shy away from the production of too many large, expensive chassis. The model that Renault did design for the luxury trade was targeted at the export market, especially the American market.

Renault began to import his thirty-five horsepower, four-cylinder chassis to the United States in 1909, opening a "selling branch" on New York's Fifth Avenue. Raffalovich's victory with just such a machine in the New York 24-Hour Race of that year provided timely and valuable publicity. Even though Renault never achieved its first-year American sales goal of 1200 to 1500 chassis, a heartening number of buyers were impressed by the model's moderate size and easy handling. During the years before the outbreak of World War I a considerable number of Renault chassis, bodied as limousines, proceeded along the streets of New York and other Eastern cities.

Renault's four-cylinder, thirty-five horsepower engine had an illustrious pedigree, having been conceived by Viet, the master designer who came to Renault Frères from DeDion-Bouton. It was the product of the lessons learned in capturing great victories in the Paris-Toulouse, Paris-Bordeaux and Paris-Vienna races. The 35 horsepower model also enjoyed the benefit of Louis Renault's most inspired and lucrative innovations: the detachable spark plugs and hydraulic shock absorbers that he invented, and the carburetor and conical clutch he perfected.

Technically, the four-cylinder Renault made an excellent luxury car, embodying one of its manufacturer's guiding principles, which historian Yves Richard has summarized in the following way: "Power is not everything, and . . . real efficiency is only obtained by using the available power to the full, by means of a light, robust structure." The chassis was light and maneuverable; it was also sturdy and dependable. Indeed, an advertisement described the Renault, with some justice, as "the car that will last forever." If the Renault was unlikely to subject its owner to inconvenient and embarrassing malfunctions, it also had the virtue of being a quiet car. This was guaranteed by the single-sleeve exhaust combined with an overhead intake poppet valve that the master of Billancourt perfected, amid an atmosphere of ferocious international competition, in 1908.

The four-cylinder 1911 Renault CF limousine pictured here has a displacement of 520.9 cubic inches. It can develop 35-45 horsepower and can attain a speed of 60 miles per hour. Its wheelbase is 147.5 inches, and the initial chassis cost was $7,500 F.O.B. New York.

It was bodied by Brewster & Company, at that time the oldest coachbuilder in the United States. Brewster was certainly one of the preeminent American manufacturers of carriages and automobile bodies, and many authorities have called it the finest. The firm captured the Grand Prize and several special awards in the French International Exposition of 1878, and subsequently won top honors in a number of domestic competitions. Company stationery carried the motto "Carriage Builders to American Gentlemen," and

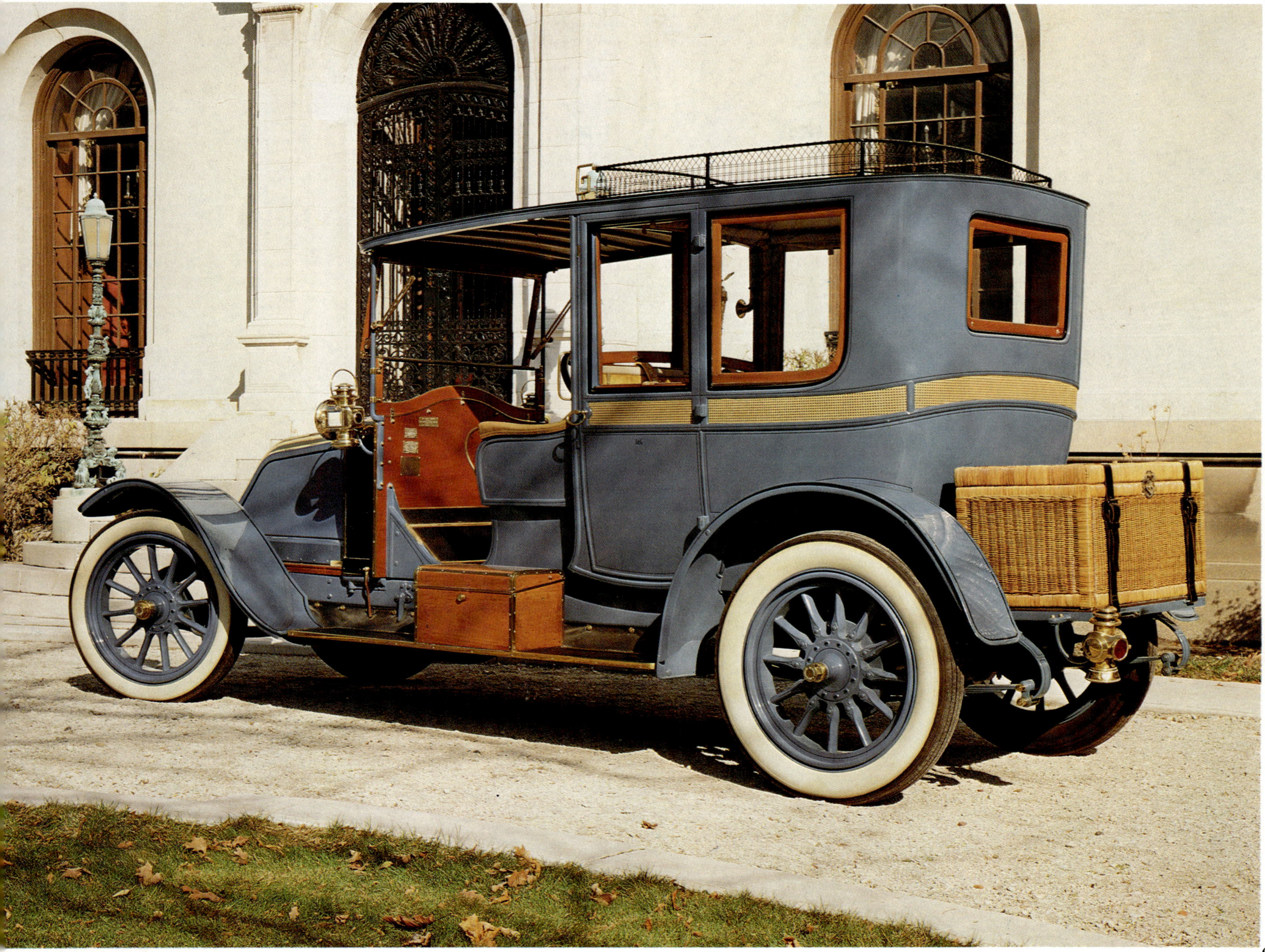

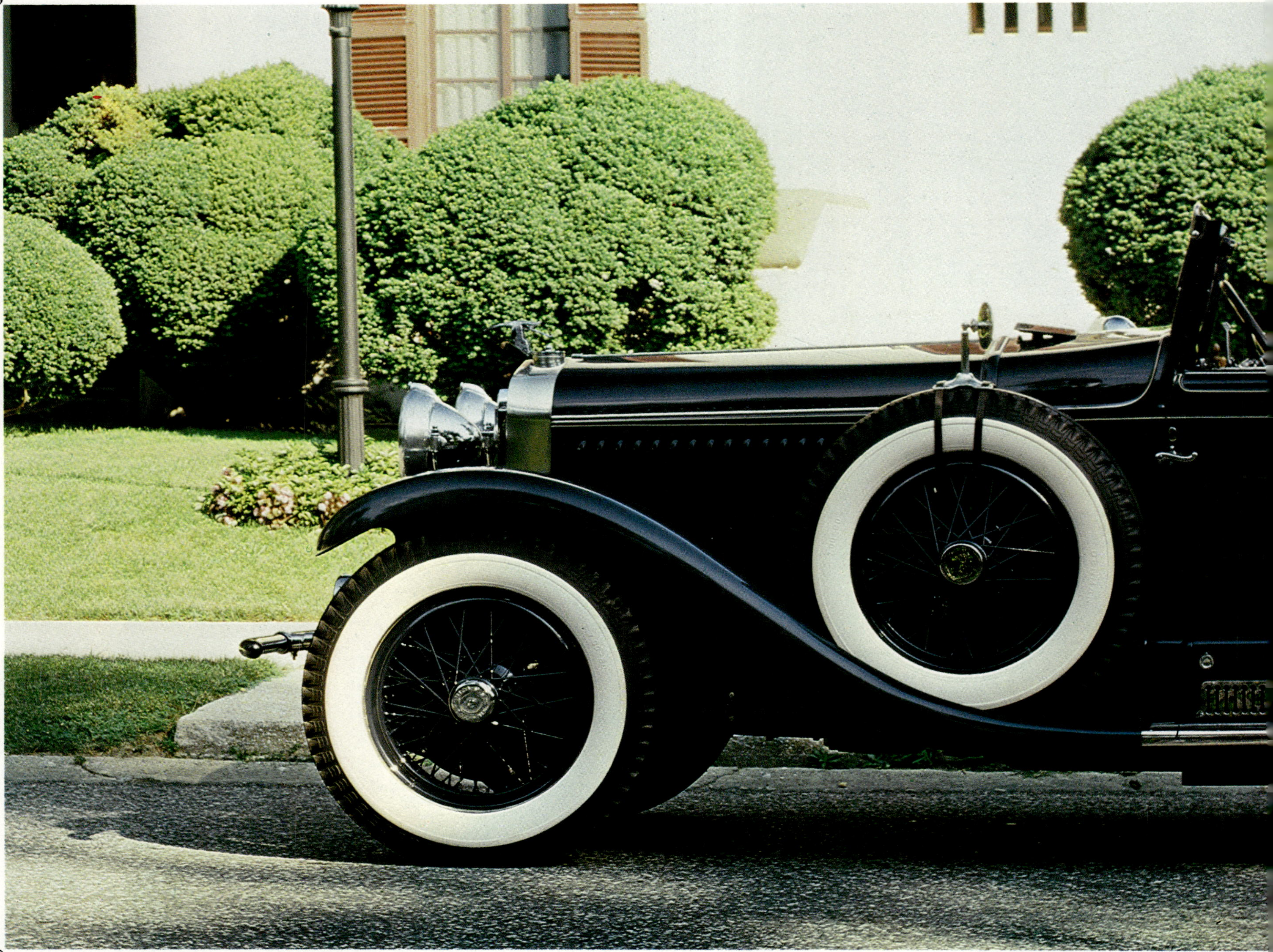

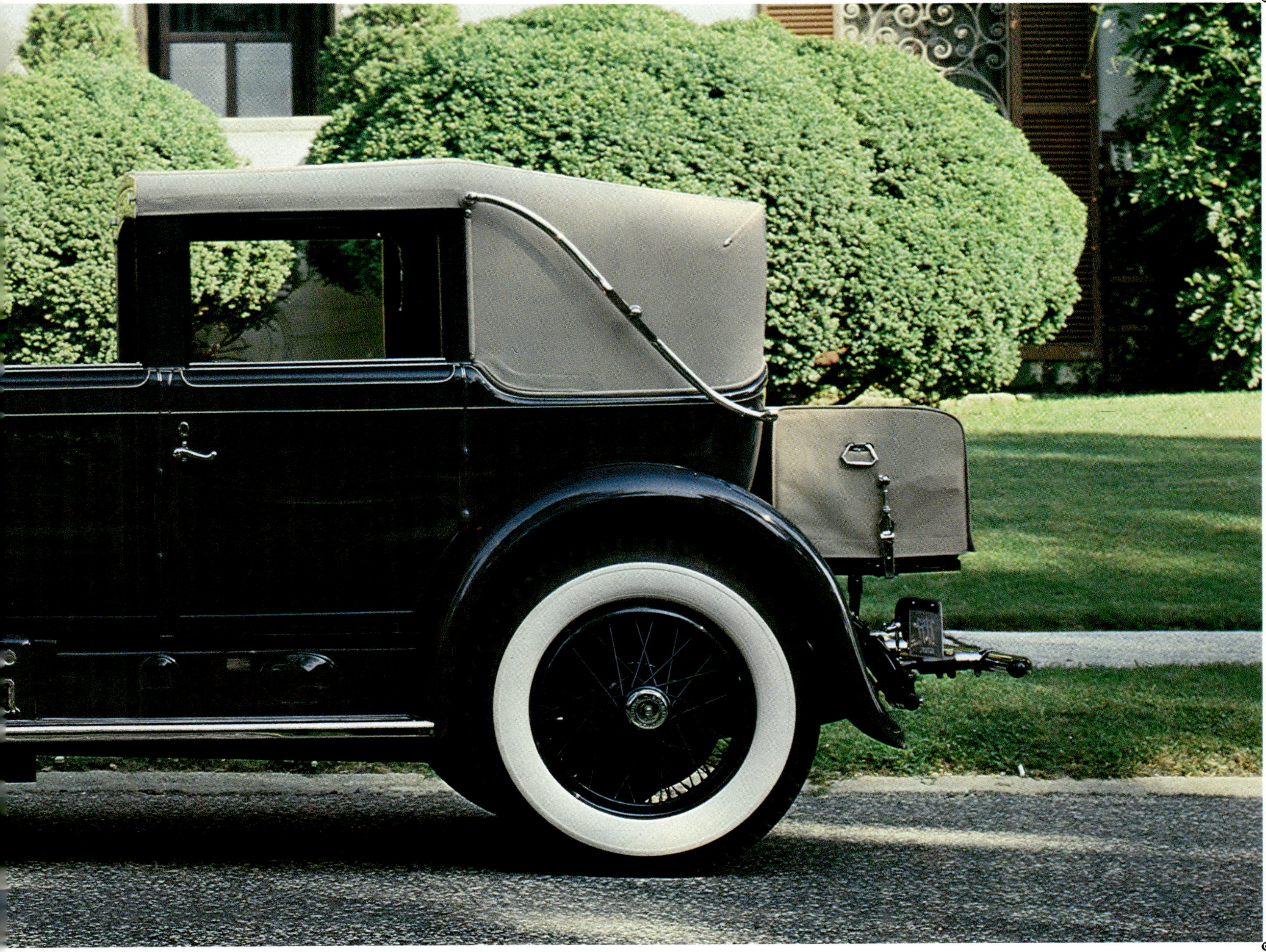

the firm's order book for the fiscal year ending in March 1882 included such illustrious names as John Jacob Astor, J. Pierpont Morgan, J.R. Roosevelt, William Rockefeller, Leland Stanford and Ulysses S. Grant.

During the years after World War I Brewster, relocated in 1910 from Manhattan to Long Island City, was noted for the conservative elegance of its bodywork. Many Brewster bodies were black or a soft gray; others were a rich, deep shade of green developed by the company and called "Brewster Green." Traditionally, the surface of Brewster bodywork was flawless; company president William Brewster was famous for his early morning rounds of inspection, during which he produced a penknife or half dollar and scored any shoddily painted panels he might find with a disfiguring "X." Interiors were similarly subdued and equally masterful. The firm's specially-made hardware was either left with its natural bronze finish or painted to harmonize with the car's dark upholstery. In each case the objective was to make the fittings as unobtrusive as possible. Upholstery was often pleated but otherwise unornamented, and Brewster scorned the extensive use of elaborate wood paneling favored by most other luxury coachbuilders of the day.

But a more flamboyant taste prevailed during Brewster's first years as an automotive coachbuilder, at the time that the Renault limousine pictured in this article was completed. Whether this ornamental exuberance owed something to the lingering influence of William Brewster's *bon vivant* father Henry, "the best dressed fat man in America," or whether it was simply due to carriage building fashions of the last quarter of the Nineteenth Century, the first Brewster automobile bodies were as brightly colored and their interiors as sumptuous as were those of the great coachbuilders of Europe. This love of bright color and intricate ornamentation is well evidenced by the 1911 Renault CF limousine.

Roy Lindsay, European correspondent for *The Horseless Age*, reported to his readers on the Olympia and Paris auto shows during the years prior to the outbreak of the First World War. His concern, and presumably that of his readers, was not so much with the mechanical evolution of luxury cars or with their overall lines, as it was with details of styling and, especially, with interior design. "Profuse and beautiful decoration" always caught his eye, and he devoted rhapsodic paragraphs to describing silk brocade upholstery, spring blinds, leather door pockets and ceilings dignified with appliqué work. In reporting on one limousine interior he observed that "satinwood tables, brass hat rack, coat hangers, a very complete lady's dressing case, liquour and spirit bottles and glasses, together with a luxuriously fitted luncheon equipment make the passengers almost independent of hotel accommodation."

The Renault limousine featured here embodies the same conspicuous luxury celebrated in Lindsay's dispatches. Thanks to the meticulous restoration undertaken by the car's former owner, Thomas J. Lester, one notices immediately the finely finished brass headlamps, taillamps and trim, and the mahogany dash, tool box and decoration. The wicker basket/trunk, with its elaborately figured oriental clasp, is a replica that serves as a reminder of Brewster's extensive use of carefully worked natural materials.

Canework side panels were another Brewster trademark. Occasionally, as in the case of this Renault limousine, the decoration was made from genuine cane. But because the material deteriorated so quickly, it was more common to use simulated cane. This artificial French canework was painted onto body panels in a thick layer, so that the final product resembled the natural material in texture as well as color. None but the most accomplished painters could do the intricate striping that the process required, and Brewster was one of only two or three American coachbuilders to maintain several of these skilled craftsmen on the permanent payroll.

By 1911 standard interior equipment on Brewster luxury cars included a coat rail, memo book, cigarette case, scent bottle, mirror box, card case, hat brush, vase and holder, watch and rug. The tufted leather chauffeur's seat and the brocaded and velvet interior of the passenger compartment of the Renault CF limousine pictured here were typical Brewster interior treatments.

William Brewster, who inherited his grandfather's admiration of Benjamin Franklin's maxims, conducted his business with austere integrity. When his firm was bought out by Rolls-Royce in 1925 and techniques of mass production began to be applied even to the manufacture of luxury automobiles, he chose to resign his position. His well-known letter of resignation dating from 1927 reflects the love of the gracious, the orderly and the seemly that his finest luxury cars embody. "I once discharged four of our best workmen simply because they would not say good morning to me on my rounds and seemed to be generally grouchy," he wrote. "Many years ago I let our chief man in the office go, not because he was incompetent, but because he always expressed such sordid mean views in any discussion that came up that he took the joy out of living...."

The First World War and the financial and technological changes that followed from it had a massive and initially beneficial effect upon the luxury car market. No cars bear more conspicuously the mark of the war than do the Hispano-Suiza H6 models, variations of which were produced between 1919 and the mid-Thirties. While no more than 2614 chassis in the H6 series were produced—perhaps a quarter of these were exported to the United States—their impact was profound. Strother MacMinn has epitomized the judgment of other authorities in calling this Hispano concept "the most innovative and significant design of the decade."

The Hispano-Suiza H6 bore one immediately noticeable reminder of The Great War, the French sculptor Bazin's *cigogne volante*, or flying stork. This distinctive mascot was a memorial both to French air ace Captain Georges Guynemer, whose Spad bore a flying stork badge, and to all Allied air heroes. The gracefully sculpted bird made its first appearance at the Paris Automobile Salon of 1919 and immediately won the admiration of commentators, designers and purchasers of luxury cars. For British novelist and playwright Michael Arlen, author of *The Green Hat* (1924), Hisso's distinctive mascot symbolized the power, beauty, spirit and mystique of the entire car. "Flying over the crest of this great bonnet," Arlen wrote, "as though in proud flight over the heads of phantom horses, was that silver stork by which the gentle may be pleased to know that they have just escaped death beneath the wheels of a Hispano-Suiza car, as supplied to His Most Catholic Majesty."

Beneath the "great bonnet" was an even more significant reminder of the First World War, the engine of the H6. In 1914 Marc Birkigt, Hispano-Suiza's chief engineer and presiding genius, based himself at the company's new French factory at Bois-Colombes, where he dedicated himself to developing aircraft engines for the Allied air forces. Indeed, Birkigt's engine was so successful that it was the father of more than 50,000 aircraft engines built between the beginning of World War I and the close of World War II.

It also formed the basis for Hispano's postwar automobile engine. Essentially, the H6 engine consisted of one bank of a prototype V-12 aircraft engine; its exterior resembled Nieuport and Spad powerplants. The single overhead camshaft was driven by a vertical shaft and bevel gears. Externally threaded, nitrided steel bores were screwed into the aluminum cylinder block. A secret process of high-pressure black enameling protected the block from corrosion. The seven-bearing crankshaft was machined from a solid billet of the finest forged steel, which was reduced in weight from six hundred to one hundred pounds in the process. Displacement was 6597 cc with a 100 mm bore and 140 mm stroke. The compression ratio was 4.5:1, and power output was 135 bhp at 3000 rpm. Low range output was a magisterial 100 bhp at 1000 rpm.

The distinctive instrument cluster of the H6 Hispano series betrayed its origins in the aviation field. The sound of the H6's engine also recalled its ancestry; Birkigt thought it entirely appropriate that an automobile engine should make itself heard during slow running. Michael Arlen described the Hispano's vocal range as beginning with a "whirring" and ending in "cruel screams."

The H6B, of which the town car featured here is an example, was the second of three models within the H6 series, and was produced in France between 1924 and 1928. The chassis wheelbase was 145.25 inches; its weight was 2500 pounds. During the Twenties, the Hispano-Suiza was the most expensive chassis produced in Europe, costing in the $14,500 range.

The great proportion of chassis in the H6 series were bodied by Kellner, Saoutchik, Labourdette, Van den Plas or Hibbard & Darrin on the Continent, or by Brewster or DeDietrich in the United States. The 1928 H6B Hispano-Suiza Cabriolet de Ville pictured here was bodied by Hibbard & Darrin of the Rue de Berri and then the Champs Elysées in Paris. Built for Seymour Knox of East Aurora, New York, a suburb of Buffalo, this town car exemplifies the elegant yet modern design that made the young firm of Hibbard & Darrin the sensation of the 1928 Paris Salon and an internationally respected house during the period from 1923 to 1931.

The late Howard "Dutch" Darrin has described the situation that he and his partner Thomas L. Hibbard discovered when the two young Americans first formed their partnership. "In Paris at that time there was what might be called a vacuum caused by four years of war, and lack of capital and many other things, and the automobile coachbuilding business had not recovered. Also, the old ideas still held forth.... We actually weren't very experienced, but we had one thing in our favor—our way of thinking. We thought ideas should be young and numerous old customs disregarded.... Never, never had such an opportunity been given anyone." (See article in AUTOMOBILE *Quarterly*, Volume VII, Number 1.)

At the beginning of their partnership, Hibbard and Darrin concentrated almost exclusively upon designing innovative bodies for the technically excellent, reasonably priced Minerva chassis. These designs—which were rendered almost exclusively by Thomas Hibbard, in 1920 a co-founder of New York's LeBaron design firm—were then executed by the leading coachbuilders in Belgium, usually Van den Plas or d'Ieteren Frères. Eventually Hibbard & Darrin diversified their operations and designed bodies for other high-grade chassis, especially for Rolls-Royce, Hispano-Suiza, Excelsior and Isotta Fraschini. And soon, thanks to a loan from one of their customers, the youthful partners were able to reduce their travel time and ensure quality control by establishing their own coachbuilding facilities in Puteaux, a suburb of Paris.

Nearly all of Hibbard & Darrin's creations were intended to be chauffeur-driven; few of their bodies were completely enclosed. About half of the firm's customers were Americans. Some requested that, upon completion, their automobiles be shipped directly to the United States, while others used their new cars while touring or living on the Continent. Buyers, whether prosperous North Americans, Argentinians or Europeans, were fascinated by the way in which the new firm ignored some conventions of the luxury coachbuilding trade, observed others, and nevertheless produced harmonious bodies that were attractive in both aesthetic and practical terms.

The lines of most Hibbard & Darrin bodies were rounded, and the firm's creations bore little resemblance to the angular, boxy bodies that were derived more directly from the carriage tradition. On the other hand, the company shied away from the sober color schemes favored by such esteemed automobile builders as Barker and Brewster, and

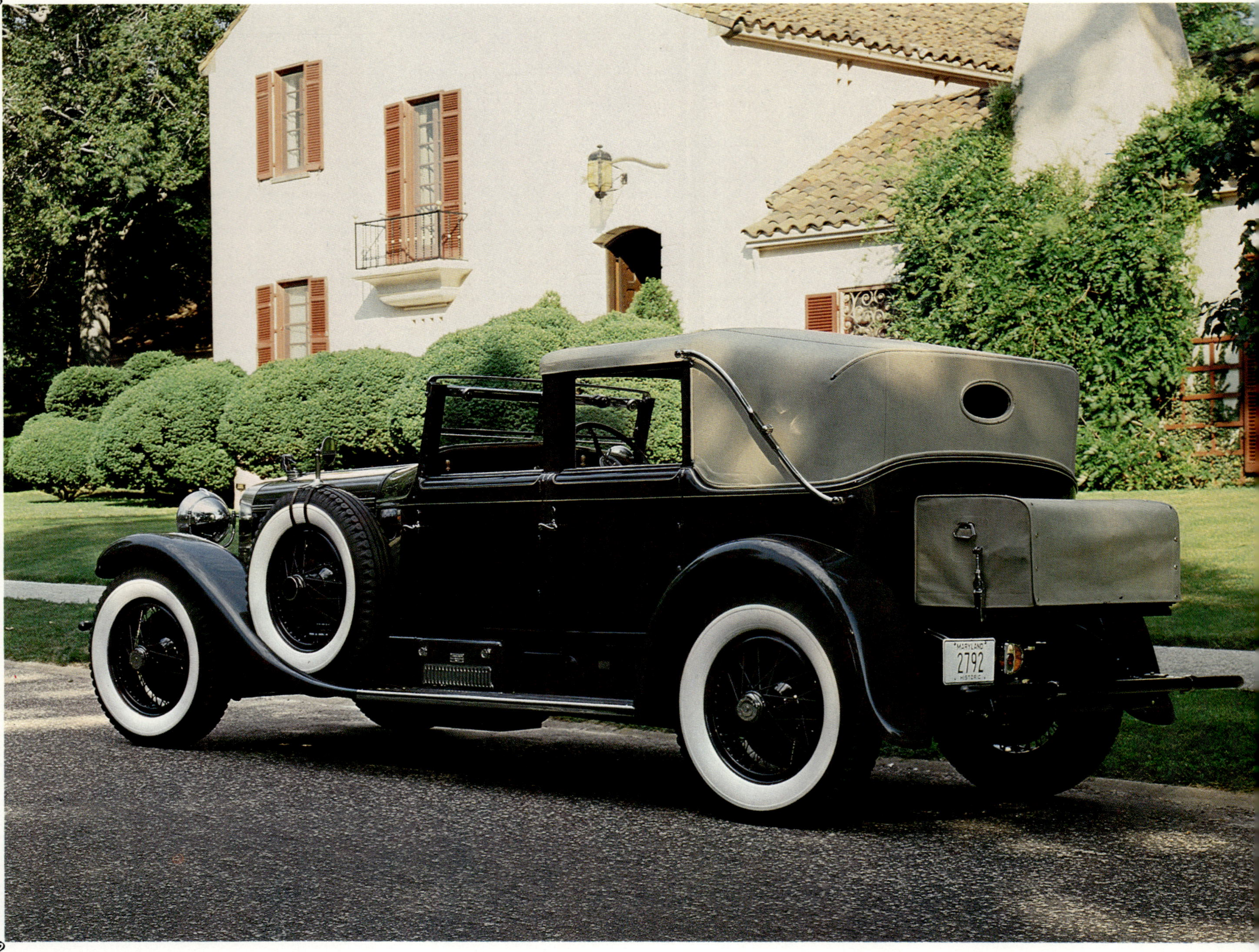
MARYLAND
2792
HISTORIC

specialized in the brighter, more distinctively colored bodies characteristic of the carriage age. While Hibbard & Darrin produced almost no black or maroon bodies and few dark blue ones—the salon car pictured here is a lovely exception to this generalization—they built large numbers of tile red, yellow and sandy beige cars. Thomas Hibbard recalls that one of the company's loveliest colors was "Almond," a pale green-gray shade.

Hibbard & Darrin also adopted a distinctive moulding treatment that appeared on many of their bodies. This consisted of a moulding about an inch in width that began at the radiator and, growing progressively wider, ran back against the side of the hood. It divided on the cowl, and a thin strip ran in front of the windshield, while the main portion of the moulding continued along the door, encircling the whole body. In the case of Seymour Knox's Hispano-Suiza town car, the body moulding was an ivory shade.

Again, the interior of Hibbard & Darrin bodies displayed a curious combination of traditional and more modern elements. The firm's cabinet-makers produced interior panels, instrument boards, vanity cases and compartments that were as finely crafted as were the creations of the most traditional luxury coachbuilders. But Hibbard & Darrin avoided their rich combination of woods, using walnut veneers almost exclusively. Later, their craftsmen turned more and more to less obtrusive paneling that was painted a solid color to match the rich but unpatterned fabrics used for the interior upholstery.

The firm's interiors were equipped with the glass and metal fittings that were a customary complement to luxury car passenger compartments: mirrors, pin and scent bottles, regulator handles, pull-to handles, door handles, switch plates, robe rails and mountings, and dome and reading lights. Often the same modern design motif appeared on each of these objects.

Hibbard & Darrin developed two distinctive top treatments. Howard Darrin devised a convertible phaeton in which a triangular section of the top material came down to close the gap between trapezoidal door windows. The firm also refined Barker & Company's fully convertible driver's compartment for closed cars. This feature consisted of a fold-away roof section that was stored in a compartment behind the driver's head. The extended roof, together with the windows of the car's large front doors, rendered the chauffeur's compartment entirely weatherproof. The 1928 Hispano-Suiza featured here has been fitted with a variation of this arrangement, and thus it can serve as a fully enclosed sedan, an open-front town car or a fully open tourer.

In "Body Design and Construction in Europe," a well-known paper that he read to the Society of Automotive Engineers in 1930, Thomas Hibbard praised the flexibility and inventiveness of the great European coachbuilders, who often adopted ingenious solutions to deal with unique circumstances. The H6B built for Seymour Knox is a case in point. Since the car was intended for use in an area that suffered severe winters, Hibbard & Darrin fitted the body with a special manually operated louvered winter radiator shell.

Because so many of Hibbard & Darrin's customers lived in countries with extreme climates, and consequently were concerned about the longevity of their cars' all-wooden frameworks, the partners investigated the possibility of constructing metal-reinforced bodies. By 1929 they had developed the process called "Sylentlyte," whereby most automotive body sections were cast in light aluminum. Unfortunately, the "Sylentlyte" technique was really too expensive for a company that was engaged in limited production, and a combination of foundry costs, a lavishly appointed New York showroom on 57th Street between Fifth and Madison Avenues and the progress of the Depression led, in 1931, to the dissolution of Hibbard & Darrin.

Limousines lounged softly by," observed Michael Arlen in the course of evoking a Mayfair street of 1922. It was a description that could only apply to a post-war street traveled by post-war luxury cars. However beautifully crafted and well engineered the limousines from the years before the First World War might be, it seems almost ludicrous to apply to them so casual a verb as Arlen's. The 1911 Renault limousine featured in this salon might, as befits its solid angularity, loom or even lurch, but could it move with such easy elegance that it could ever be said to lounge? On the other hand, we can easily imagine that Hibbard & Darrin's H6B Hispano-Suiza was destined not for a career of meeting dignitaries at an American railroad station and appearing in local ceremonial parades, but rather for winding in leisurely fashion along the streets of one of the European capitals. ✥

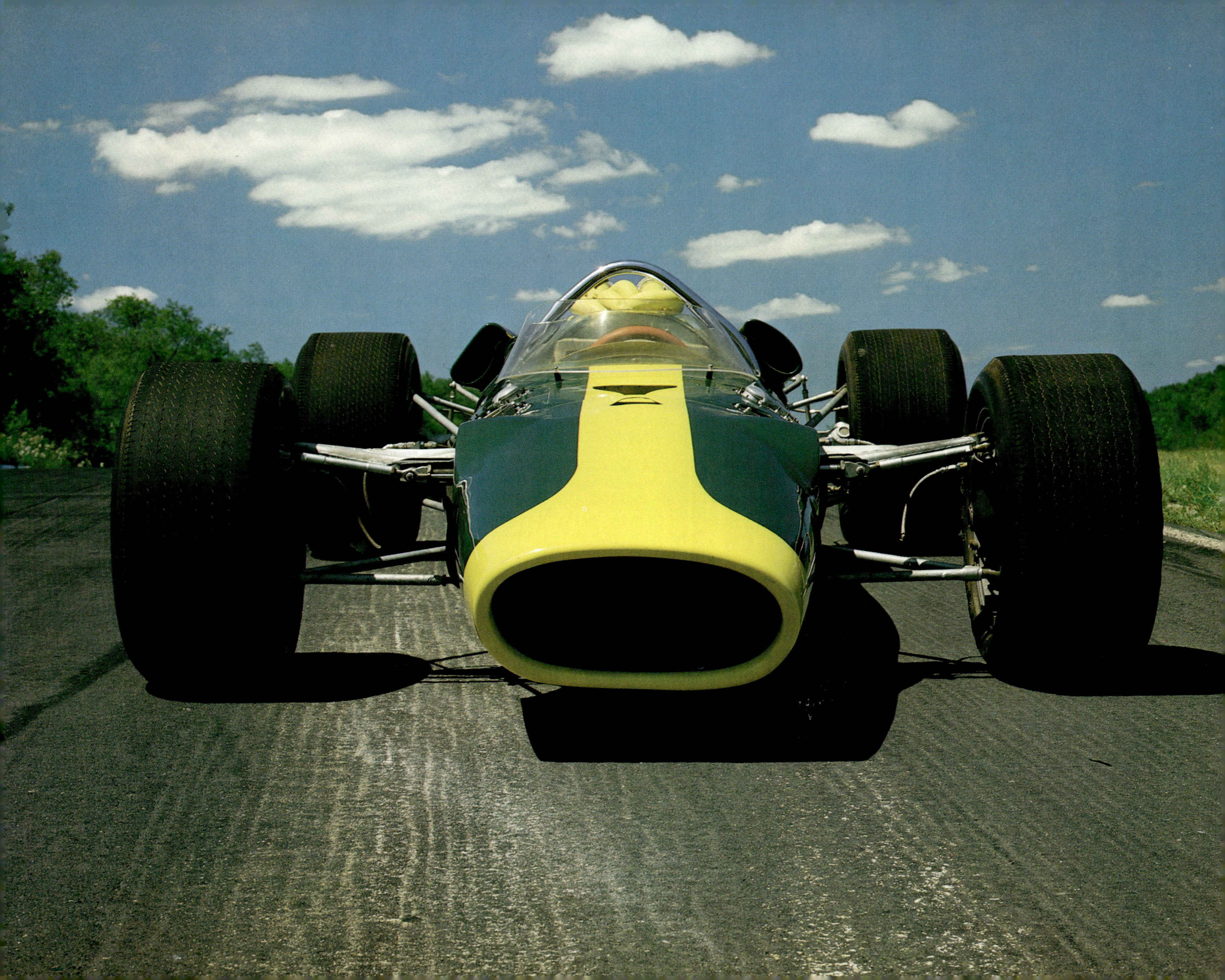

## JIM HAYNES AND HIS MYSTERY LOTUS

# STALKING A CHAMPION

## By Ed Morley

Readers of AUTOMOBILE *Quarterly* are familiar with the exhaustive detective work that reconstructing automotive history often requires. The historian of the automobile finds himself piecing together the past by interviewing surviving relatives and friends of legendary figures, sifting through yellowing documents in courthouses and patent offices, and visiting graveyards on farms and in remote country parishes.

Of course, all questions of automotive history do not involve the moldering, tarnish-covered past; some matters of authentication and verification concern automobiles and automotive events of very recent years. Lime Rock Park's Jim Haynes has recently shared with us just such a contemporary mystery—whatever happened to the Lotus 38 that Jimmy Clark drove to victory in the 1965 Indianapolis 500?

The question might seem ludicrous, given the enormous publicity surrounding Clark's triumph with that technological marvel built by Lotus from a design by Len Terry, and powered by a Ford quad-cam V-8 engine. Yet it was only after exhaustive investigation that Haynes was able to say with certainty that the "old Indianapolis car" he found advertised in *AutoWeek* and bought in Kansas City in 1970 was, indeed, the 1965 winner.

Only gradually did Haynes and his associates sort out the complex fortunes of the Lotus 38 between the years 1965 and 1970. There were several causes for the prevailing confusion: six Lotus 38's were eventually built, the cars changed hands frequently, were subjected to painting and repainting, and met with a variety of modifications and disasters. To make things even more problematic, the half-dozen Lotus 38's were never officially numbered in series, although Haynes and his colleagues adopted such a system of numeration in the course of their research, one that we will follow for the sake of clarity.

At the beginning of the 1965 season there were three Lotus 38's—Jimmy Clark's 38/1, Roger McCluskey's 38/2 and Dan Gurney's 38/3. During testing in Trenton, New Jersey that April, McCluskey's car crashed and was destroyed. At that point the Lotus 38/4 was built for the use of Bobby Johns.

Jimmy Clark came to the 1965 Indianapolis 500 with two frustrating

## Photography by Roy Query

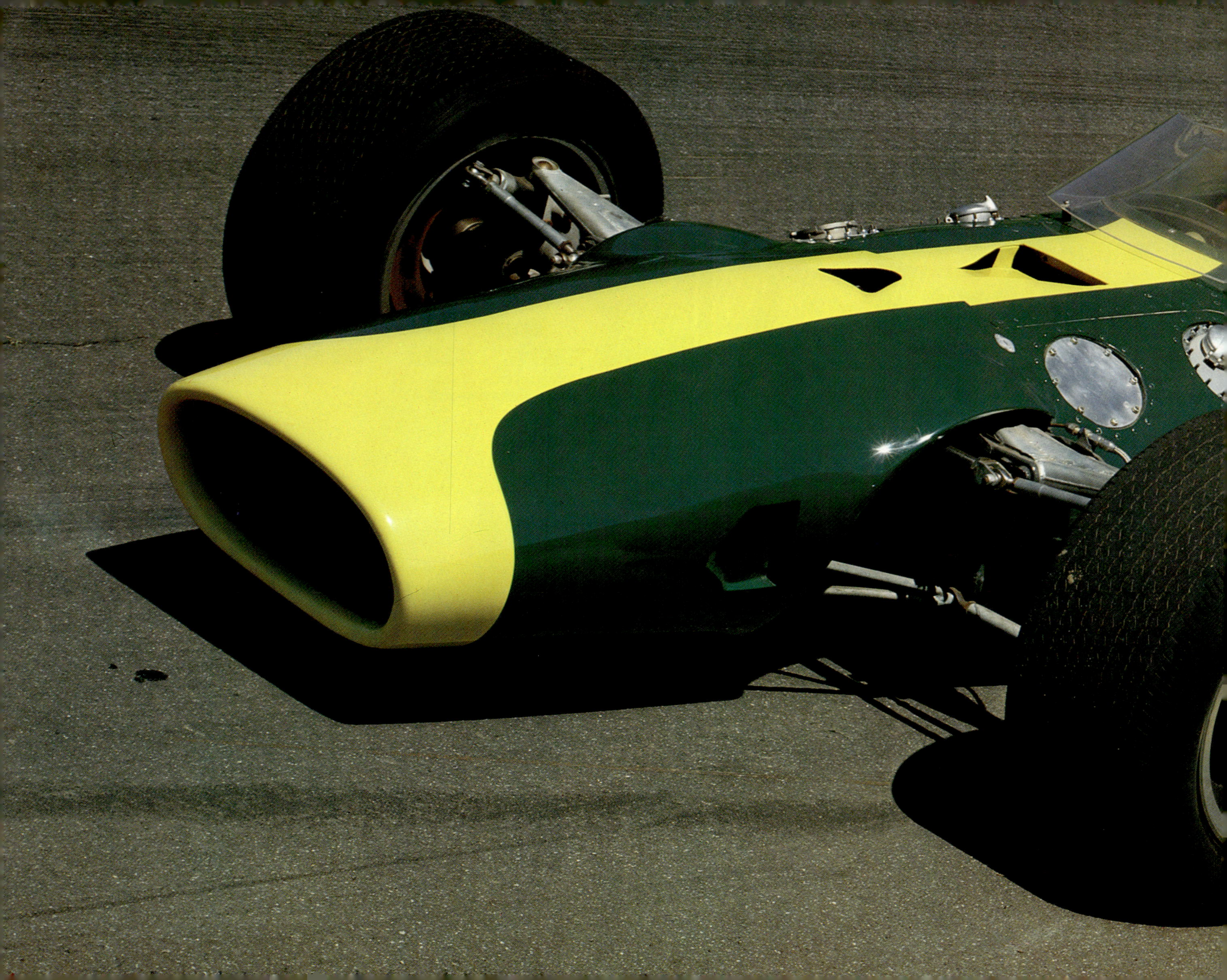

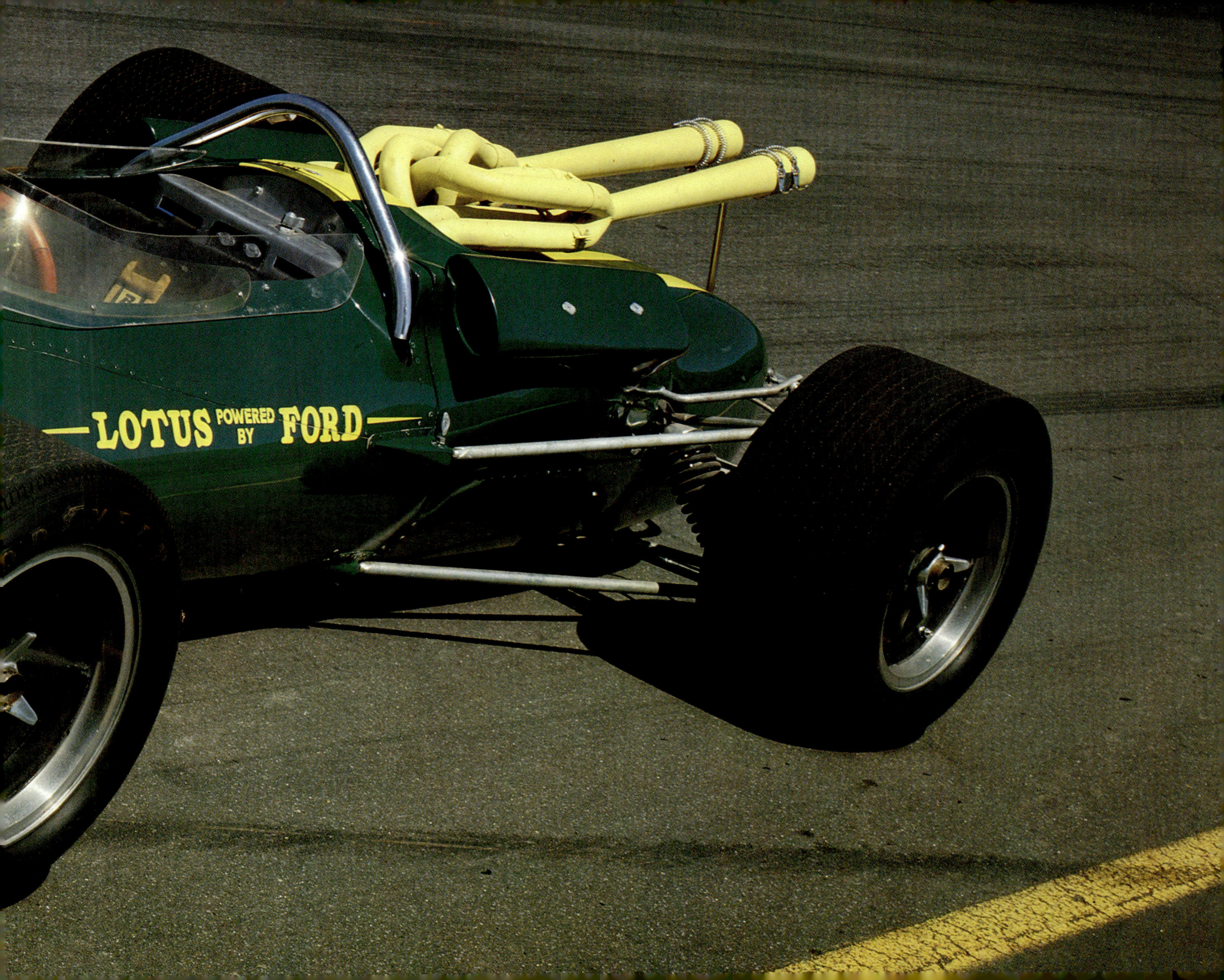
LOTUS POWERED BY FORD

defeats behind him. During the '63 contest he had led the field for twenty-eight laps, but finished second to Parnelli Jones in a front-engined Offy after the track became slick with oil. In the next contest Clark was ahead until his tires began to lose their tread and his suspension failed.

During the preliminaries for 1965's 500, Jimmy Clark in his new Lotus 38 qualified at 160.729 mph, thus becoming the first man to break 160, although A.J. Foyt would out-perform him a few hours later with a four-lap average of 161.233. But no one managed to better Clark during the actual race. The Lotus-Ford effort had had refueling problems in 1963 and '64, and brought in the Wood Brothers stock car team to guarantee that the costly delays would not recur. They loaded 50 gallons of fuel in 19.8 seconds during Clark's first stop, and 58 more in 24.7 seconds during the second.

By then the outcome seemed reassuringly certain, and at the end Clark had led for all but ten laps of the race, and came away with $166,000 of the $628,000 prize money. Parnelli Jones was second in a Lotus 34 and Mario Andretti was third in a Brabham. Bobby Johns came in seventh with his 38/4, while the 38/3 suffered engine failure and Gurney was forced to drop out of the race.

After the 38/1's spectacular Indy performance, two more 38's were quickly built for A.J. Foyt (38/5) and Mario Andretti (38/6). These two late arrivals were called "Soft Alloy Specials," since their bodies were made from soft aluminum rather than high tensile alloy sheet. Lacking in rigidity, Foyt's 38/5 was demolished in the eleven-car smashup that inaugurated the 1966 Indy 500, while Andretti chose to use his 38/6 only as a backup, eventually selling it to Gordon van Liew.

As another consequence of the 1965 Indy 500, one of the four hard alloy Lotuses was placed in the Ford Museum to memorialize the company's role in the victory. Which 38 was it? The 38/1 in which Clark actually triumphed, or Johns' look-alike 38/4? From the outset of his investigations Haynes suspected that the car leading the safe if unadventurous life of a museum piece was the 38/4, but it was only later that he found material evidence for his theory.

Haynes' attempts to verify the suspicion that his Lotus was Clark's 38/1 began, then, with few certainties. Since routine tests revealed that his was one of the quartet of high tensile cars, he could immediately eliminate 38/5 and 38/6 from contention. And as 38/2 had been reduced to debris in the spring of 1965, it too could be dismissed. So the question was at once elementary and baffling: was he the owner of the 38/1, the 38/3 or the 38/4?

As mentioned above, one Lotus went to the Ford Museum after the '65 Indy contest, while another went on the Champ trail with Clark. At Indianapolis in 1966 Clark suffered tire problems and spun out three times in his 38, coming in second to Graham Hill's newer Lotus 42F. Al Unser was also an unsuccessful competitor at the '66 event, driving the 38/3 that he had acquired from Gurney. Since they were running under the sponsorship of Andy Granatelli's STP Corporation, both 38's, formerly green, had been painted a Day-Glo orange.

After the disappointing Indianapolis finish in 1966, the car Clark had used—either the 38/1 or the 38/4—was sold to A.J. Foyt and painted white, Sheraton-Thompson's color. Shortly thereafter Foyt crashed the car and sold it to one of his associates, Jerry Crew. When the necessary repairs had been made, Crew had the Lotus painted gold and finally, in 1970, sold it to Haynes. (Jimmy Clark, incidentally, had one more try at the Indianapolis 500 in 1967, with the Lotus 38/3 originally driven in 1965 by Dan Gurney. Because of engine failure he placed thirty-first.)

When Jim Haynes and his restorer, Pete Magnusen of Falls Village, Connecticut, examined the Lotus that had just been purchased from Crew, they found a revealing succession of paint schemes: Lotus green directly on top of the metal, then S.T.P. Day-Glo orange, Sheraton-Thompson white, and finally, Crew's gold. From the testimony of the paint Haynes knew he had bought the Lotus 38 that Clark had driven at Indy in 1966, and which had then passed to Foyt and to Crew. But what he still did not know was whether it was the 38/1 that had been triumphant the previous year, or merely the 38/4. Were there, he wondered, any documented structural differences that would conclusively distinguish the 38/1 from the 38/4?

Haynes found what he was seeking when he dug deeper into the history of the 38's development. As *Ford: The Dust and the Glory* explains, Parnelli Jones was practicing in his Lotus 34 for the 1965 Indianapolis 500 when a rear upright broke for the second time. Since a similar flaw affected another Lotus, the USAC safety committee grounded all Lotuses pending the resolution of the problem. While Colin Chapman asserted that the weakness was found only on older cars, the safety committee insisted that every Lotus should have stronger uprights. Accordingly, a hasty pattern modification led to heavier cast uprights for the Gurney (38/3) and Johns (38/4) cars, while Clark's 38/1 was fitted with a unique, welded set. Haynes has the photographic evidence to prove that his Lotus has these specially welded uprights, and that he is, indeed, the owner of the champion 38/1.

It was one thing to authenticate the Lotus and another to restore it. Recovering the 38/1's original engine was impossible, since it had been sent back to Ford for repairs and modifications after each race during the 1965-66 period. "Odds are that the engine Clark won with doesn't even exist any more," observed Haynes. "It would just be different pieces in different engines." Nevertheless, Jim Haynes' diligence was rewarded again when he traced a never-used four-cam Ford to the home of a former Indy mechanic. There, under a glass top, it was serving as a coffee table. Along with the mint engine, which was dyno-certified for 505 hp, came a number of irreplaceable banana exhausts.

Before he decided to sell his Indy car, Jerry Crew had intended to transform it into a Formula 500 machine. Haynes, on the other hand, decided to restore it to its 1965 glory. Those readers who compare color photographs of the 38/1 taken in 1965 with Roy Query's photos from the summer of 1981 will see just how well he has succeeded. ✦

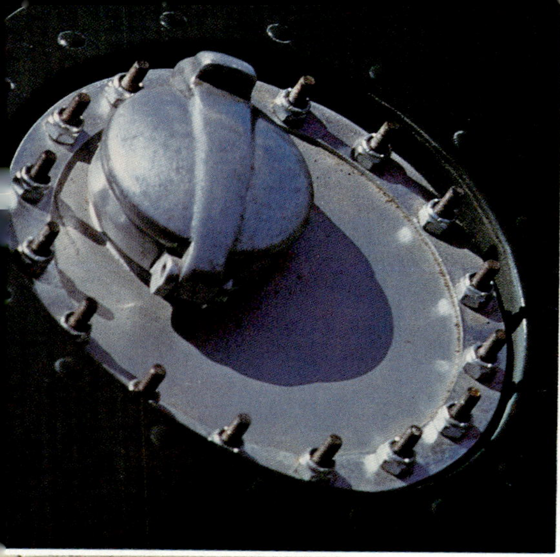

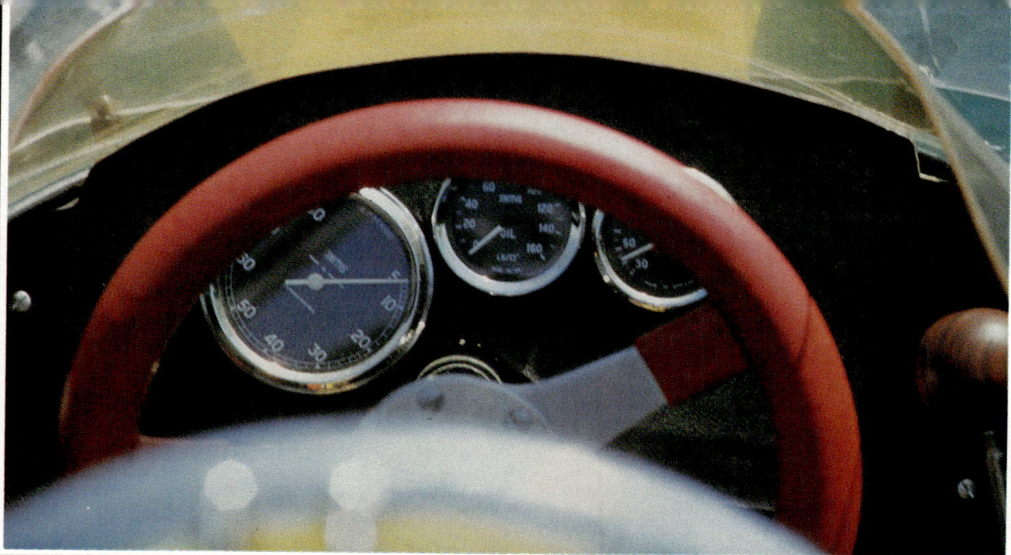

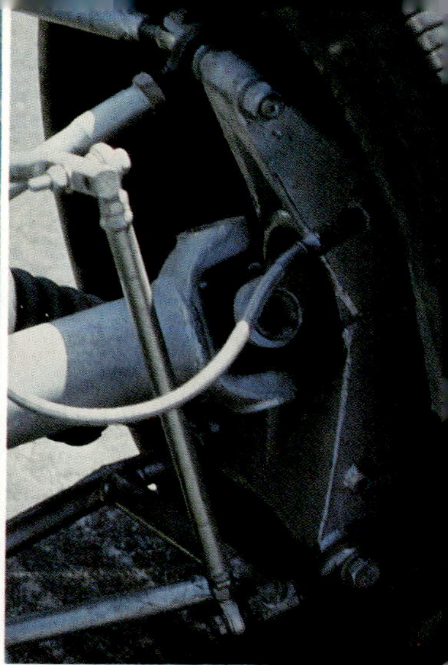

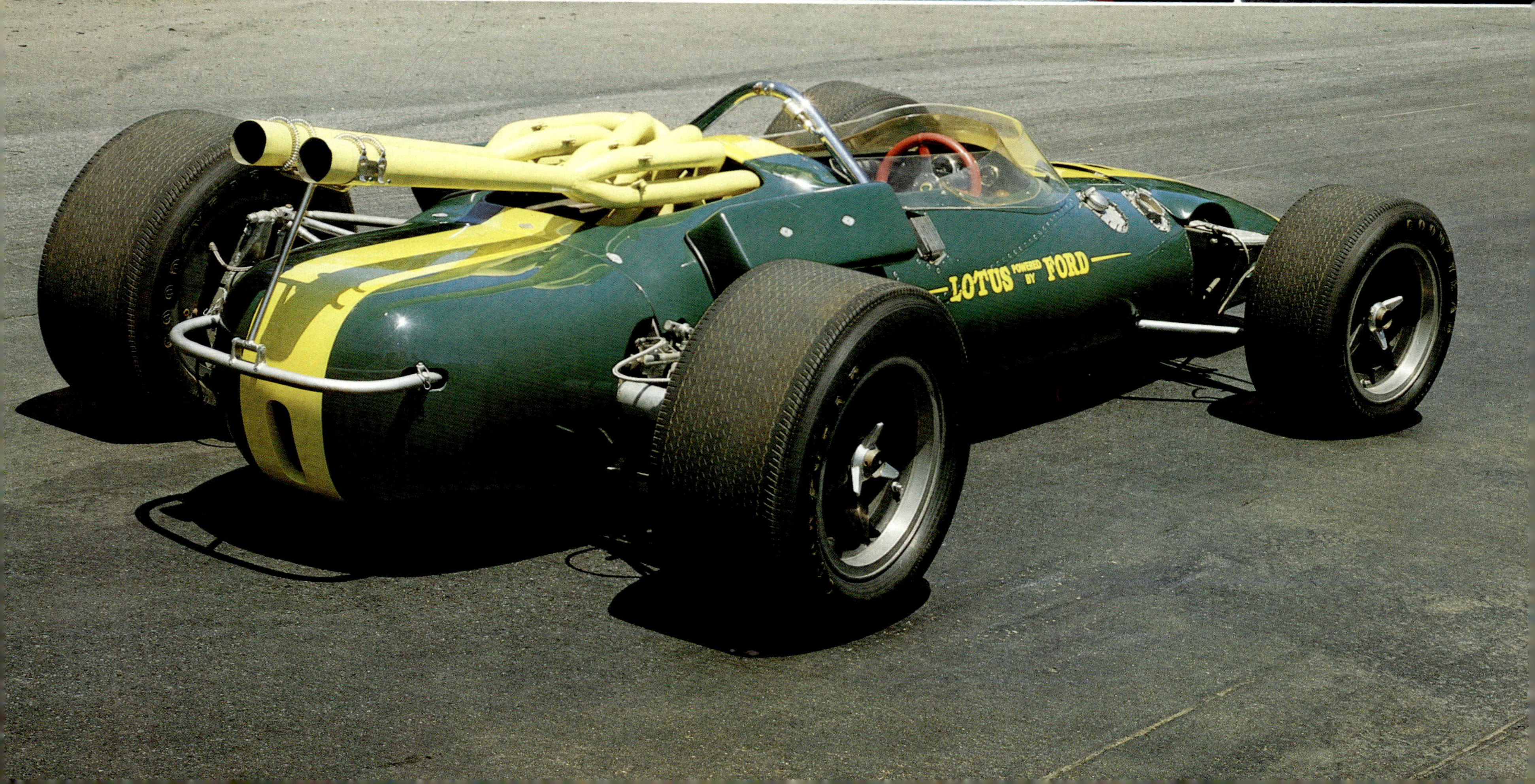
LOTUS POWERED BY FORD

# NOTES & PH

DAN BURGER served, from 1979 through 1981, as the Staff Writer for the Auburn-Cord-Duesenberg Museum in Auburn, Indiana. In that capacity he researched the Auburn Automobile Company with the help of the museum archives, through contacts with former employees of the auto manufacturer, and with the assistance of individual members of the Auburn-Cord-Duesenberg Club. One result of his efforts was the establishment of an oral history archive at the museum. While at the A-C-D Museum, Burger wrote and edited the museum newsletter, *The Accelerator*, as well as contributing articles to the *A-C-D Club Newsletter* and publications such as *AutoWeek, Antique Automobile* and *Cars & Parts*. He is a member of the Society of Automotive Historians and the Indiana Historical Society. Presently he is employed as a free-lance writer while living in Southern California.

### TIP-ON
Patent drawing by Alan H. Leamy filed on January 18th, 1930 for the front wheel drive L-29 Cord. Drawing courtesy of the Auburn-Cord-Duesenberg Museum.

### FRONTISPIECE
Knox trademark plate from 1904 93 Flatbed Truck owned by Max Hofferbert. Photograph by Rick Lenz.

### CONTENTS PAGE
Exhaust pipes from Jim Haynes' 1965 Lotus 38 as photographed by Roy Query.

### KNOX
Photography by Roy Query: 116-17, 118, 124 (bottom); photography by Rick Lenz: 119 (top and bottom), 120, 121 (top and bottom), 122-23, 125, 126-27, 128, 129, 130-31. Photo courtesy of Harrah's Automobile Collection: 124 (top). For their help in lending factory literature and other documentation the author and editors would like to thank Walter Bittner and Bill Kuring.

### ALAN H. LEAMY
The lead photographs show Alan Leamy's design for a front-drive, four-place Cabin Speedster, and the designer on one of his shooting expeditions during the early Thirties.

All color and black and white photography was supplied by the Auburn-Cord-Duesenberg Museum, Auburn, Indiana. Through the generosity of Mrs. Leamy, visitors to the museum will find Alan Leamy's colored drawings on permanent display. Leamy's old office in the Auburn Automobile Company Administration Building has been restored, and is also to be found in the museum. We would like to thank Gregg Buttermore and the other members of the museum staff for their assistance in locating relevant drawings, photos and supporting documentation.

The author and editors are grateful to Mrs. Agnes G. Leamy for providing valuable, previously unpublished information about her husband's career. Thanks are also due to the following individuals: Stan Gilliland, David Henderson, Strother MacMinn, Alfred Ney and A.E. Williams.

### RUXTON
We wish to thank Doug Shinstine for his loan of advertisements and other documentation.

### PONTIAC'S GHOST CAR
As AUTOMOBILE *Quarterly*'s chief photographer, Roy Query, has recently described for us, the automotive photographer sometimes meets with unexpected challenges—such as Pontiac's transparent World's Fair Car. Roy began his photo session at seven in the morning and finished shortly before midnight. For effective illumination he required seven carefully concealed 500 watt floodlights. Some of the crises Roy endured during this marathon day were two blown fuses, several narrowly averted collisions with drivers who "didn't see" the Ghost Car, and the tendency of the car's Plexiglas panels, when exposed to the heat of the floodlights, to begin to sag.

### W.F. BRADLEY
The lead photograph on pages 162-63 shows Bradley as he appeared in 1920, having arrived on the high plateau of his long career. The photographs on pages 169 and 178 are from the collection of Griffith Borgeson. All other photographs have kindly been supplied by W.F.B.'s son, Mr. James A. Bradley. The author and editors wish to thank Mr. Bradley for all of the assistance he offered during the course of this project.

### FRANK COSTIN
The lead photograph on pages 180-81 shows Frank Costin trimming swarf from the front of the Amigo Chassis. Note the extensive bulkheads on the lower chassis sides. This photograph is reproduced by courtesy of Vauxhall Motors.

Other black and white photos have been obtained from the following sources: Costin Archives: 183, 184, 189, 191 (top, left), 197; Dr. Norbert McNamara: 191 (bottom, left); Nan Costin: 191 (right); Goodchild: 196; Chris Turner Collection: 200.

### LUXURY CARS
We thank Morton Y. Bullock and the Frederick C. Crawford Auto-Aviation Museum for providing information about the two cars featured in this story.

As was observed in this article, the Hispano-Suiza was of-

*Mrs. Leamy and Dick Saddler's newly restored L-29 Cord*

# OTO CREDITS

### L'HOMME A L'HISPANO
*by Pierre Frondaie*

WHITE, MAGNIFICENT LIKE A ROYAL BARQUE, but terrestrial and sedate upon her powerful wheels, the Hispano caught the last rays of daylight on her coachwork that seemed to be of ivory and silver. A few children, come to worship her, circled around her prudently.

The forest ringed the village. Everywhere—before, behind, to the right, to the left—the dense army of pines, at regimented intervals, in correct files, in concerted masses, seemed to await a mysterious order to send it marching toward the sea. A great silence, pulsing with deep respiration, rendered close the cries of distant owls. The night mounted in heavy waves and, in the houses, the lamps flared like great lanterns.

To the right of the machine, and scarcely longer than herself, there was a small inn. The window panes of the main room exposed the interior: a fireplace black as a pipe, hanging hams, a skinny cat on the counter. Three dray drivers ate at a table; at another two strangers from the cities dined.

They had left Bordeaux around six in the afternoon. Since then, the great thoroughbred, the beast de luxe, had perforated the landscapes. They had seen trees, trees, trees. They had put to flight the mules, the wild boar, the game birds of the lagoons. Like a projectile, they had penetrated the peaceful night. Now, they halted, twenty kilometers from Bayonne.

They came out of the inn. Deléone was fat and oily, like those supreme magistrats of Carthage who were hoisted onto elephants by means of block and tackle. George Dewalter had grace and beauty. His face, of a noble form, the sadness, but charm, of his smile and above all his eyes, his clear, soft changeable eyes, were the visible signs of his impassioned spirit. He seemed to be energetic and good, battered by the incessant debauch of being sentient. He seemed to be thirty years old and he wore the ribbon of the Légion d'Honneur. He wore it casually on his travelling coat.

Outside, the Hispano had disappeared progressively into the dusk. The chauffeur turned on her lights. Then, she radiated and, before her, one saw the endless road that went off toward Spain. In the distance, another army of pines had the air of awaiting battle.

"I wonder what I'm doing here," Dewalter said.

From the road, his companion shouted at him: "Obviously you're not still hunting buffalo. You're useful to me. That's what you're doing here."

It was his turn to take his place in the sumptuous coachwork. Dewalter smiled vaguely, confined himself to shrugging his shoulders, and kept quiet. The night, upon the mysterious land, smelled of frost and pitch. At the last houses of the village, the engines began the song of the road. Soon, the pace was steady and rhythmic like that of a train and, on each side of the powerful machine, in the direction opposed to her own, the trees seemed to fall back, holding their distance. The wind caused by the rush of speed howled in their ears like a wolf. Bayonne was traversed in a leap and the nervous odor of the sea announced the goal of their trip. Deléone and Dewalter were at Biarritz, in front of the Hôtel du Palais.

ten an object of wonder, even of veneration, to those who encountered it. It made no difference whether the car, with a mixture of menace and serenity, was coursing down a country road or sitting at a curbside in magnificent repose—the mystique was always there. In the box to the left is another celebration of the Hispano's iridescent personality, an excerpt from the beginning of Pierre Frondaie's novel, *L'Homme à l'Hispano* (1924). The translation from the French is by Griffith Borgeson.

COLOPHON: S.S.I
Color photograph by L. Scott Bailey.

BACK COVER
The Costin logo is debossed on our back cover.

ERRATA
In reading "Wayward Wayfarer: The Story of a Dodge," which appeared in Volume XVIII, Number 1, A.R. Good caught a typographical error that we missed. Mr. Good questions whether K.T. Keller's middle name was really "Thelma," saying: "My understanding is that Mr. Keller was an engineer of the suspenders and belt, pencils in his shirt pocket . . . variety, who would probably resent this aspersion on his manhood." Indeed, Keller's real middle name was "Thuma."

A more serious editorial error occurred in our Volume XIX, Number 3 story on GM's C-body cars of 1940-41. As Hendrik Kranendonk, Wayne Harrington and author Terry Boyce have pointed out, the 1940 Buick 66C Convertible and 1940 Buick 41C Sport Phaeton pictured there were B-bodies, not C-bodies. In referring to our own mistake and the manufacturer's one-time substitution of B- for C-body convertible publicity photos, Terry Boyce observed that "it almost seems like the 1940 C-body Buicks are cursed, never to have their photos appear in print."

### PRINTS AVAILABLE FROM THIS ISSUE

Back by popular request are AQ's full-size color prints, with white borders, perfect for framing. These press proofs of color photos and paintings are the same size as they appear in the magazine, but come to you on uncut proof sheets, shipped in a sturdy tube. Less than 150 sets available.

Set of all color photographs appearing in this issue, with the exception of those on pages 116-17, 120, and 126-27, is available for $14.95 for the entire set, plus $1.75 shipping and handling.

Pennsylvania residents add 6% sales tax; New Jersey residents add 5%.

To order, please send your check or money order to Automobile Quarterly—Print Department, 245 West Main Street, Kutztown, Pennsylvania 19530.

# "A NEW MODEL OF INDIVIDUALITY"

## 1935 S.S.I. AIRLINE SALOON

The fall 1934 press previews that heralded the birth of the 1935 S.S.I Airline Saloon acclaimed the new arrival as a worthy companion to the other members of the S.S. series. "It worthily carries on the S.S. reputation for gracefulness of line and well-balanced proportions," reported *The Autocar*.

The same review went on to praise the moderation that the car's designers had practiced in creating their more aerodynamic form. "Believing that the British motoring public is not yet ready to accept the rounded frontal aspect which is a feature of a few streamline designs, the manufacturers have retained the normal frontal aspect of the other models of the range, the same bold radiator design and graceful long bonnet." On the other hand, Sir William Lyons, commenting on his Airline more than forty years after its creation, described its appearance as "terribly ungainly."

Whatever the aesthetic merits of the 1935 Airline, its performance represented an improvement over that of its predecessors. All cars in the S.S. series had engines that were specially manufactured by the Standard Motor Company. For 1935 the addition of a new camshaft, higher compression head and two R.A.G. carburetors carefully synchronized meant larger reserves of power. The six-cylinder S.S.I Airline Saloon featured here, from Harrah's Automobile Collection, has an engine capacity of 2663 cc, a bore and stroke of 73 x 106 mm, and developed 70 bhp at 4000 rpm. It sold for £365.

Road holding, an acknowledged strong point in previous S.S. cars, was further improved in the 1935 models. The chassis frame was stiffer, thanks to the repositioning of members of the cross-bracing. Larger scissor-type shock absorbers gave improved action.

In the 1935 S.S. models greater comfort and convenience were major considerations. Door width was three feet nine inches, giving easy access to front and back seats, and there were ample head clearance, leg and elbow room for all four passengers. The absence of center pillars, and larger door, quarter and rear windows gave improved visibility. Rear seats were redesigned and *The Autocar* observed that "one sinks into them as into armchairs." An attractive range of body, upholstery, wheel and wing color schemes were available, and it was noted that "the comfort of the upholstery and its plain, dignified style are thoroughly in keeping with modern standards." The streamlined contour of the rear body space, visually disconcerting as some found it, increased covered space for luggage; a rubber-lined compartment in the tail lid held a set of tools.